THE PHILIPPINE CHURCH:

Growth in a Changing Society

CHURCH GROWTH SERIES

THE
PHILIPPINE CHURCH:
Growth in a Changing Society

by

ARTHUR LEONARD TUGGY

William B. Eerdmans Publishing Company
Grand Rapids, Michigan

FOREWORD

"Men exist, not as discrete individuals, but as interconnected members of some society .... The normal man is not an isolated unit but part of a whole which makes him what he is .... Consequently when we comprehend the social structure of a particular segment of the total population, we know better how churches are likely to increase and ramify through it" (*Understanding Church Growth*: 183).

In this volume Mr. Tuggy, a career missionary to the Philippines, and one of the team of researchers who has produced the notable study of current church growth in that advanced nation, seeks to comprehend a part of the social structure. He describes the family in the Philippines both in past centuries and in present times.

These are carefully documented chapters. Mr. Tuggy does not form his observations on a quick trip through the islands, but rather on what authorities — historians, anthropologists, Roman Catholics, Protestants, Filipinos, and Westerners — have written. Out of these rich sources, he constructs an authentic picture of the family in the Philippines and the part it plays in the spread of biblical faith.

I commend this volume to students of mission everywhere. Filipino ministers and missionaries in the islands will naturally derive most benefit from it; but it has a freight of meaning for Christian workers in every land. The family in Africa and Latin America is not, of course, exactly like the family in the Philippines, but it is like it nevertheless. Missionaries at work in many lands can here learn much about how the family affects the spread of the Gospel.

Donald McGavran, Dean
School of Missions and Institute of
    Church Growth
Fuller Theological Seminary
Pasadena, California

CONTENTS

PART I

THE INTRODUCTION OF ROMAN CATHOLIC CHRISTIANITY INTO THE PHILIPPINES

PART II

THE INTRODUCTION OF PROTESTANT CHRISTIANITY INTO THE PHILIPPINES

LIST OF FIGURES

PREFACE

This book was first produced as a thesis for the School of World Mission at Fuller Theological Seminary under the title "Philippine Society and Church Growth in Historical Perspective." The two major themes of this study, then, are Philippine social structure and church growth. As a church growth study, however, it does not aim to be exhaustive. The focus is more on the environment in which the church has grown during different important periods of Philippine history. A more complete Philippine-wide church growth survey is currently being conducted by a special research team of two men, one of whom is the writer.

The writer and his family have lived a total of nine years in the Philippines. Most of this time has been spent in provincial church-planting missionary work in Lucena City, Quezon Province, under the Conservative Baptist Foreign Mission Society. Familiarity with this area and with the Tagalog language has been a great help in this investigation, but may also have caused the writer to tend to see the whole of the Philippines through Tagalog eyes.

This book could not have been written without the encouragement, counsel and help of many people. I am particularly indebted to Dr. Donald A. McGavran for his many helpful suggestions during the research and writing.

My Tagalog informants, Mr. and Mrs. Remegio Gabriel and Mr. Andres Ilagan were most helpful in their detailed description of contemporary Tagalog family life.

Special thanks go to Mr. Alexander Chua of Manila for his fine work on the graphs and map. I am especially grateful to Mrs. Mary Gautschi for her careful editorial help.

Finally, I am deeply indebted to my wife, Jeannette, who has been a constant source of encouragement and who has worked so hard in typing this work, first in thesis form and then in revised form for this book.

Arthur Leonard Tuggy

9

ABBREVIATIONS

ABFMS   American Baptist Foreign Mission Society

ABMU   American Baptist Missionary Union

CBFMS   Conservative Baptist Foreign Mission Society

CBM   Conservative Baptist Mission

FEBIAS   Far Eastern Bible Institute and Seminary

OMF   Overseas Missionary Fellowship

UCCP   United Church of Christ in the Philippines

WCH   World Christian Handbook

YMCA   Young Men's Christian Association

PART I

THE INTRODUCTION OF ROMAN CATHOLIC CHRISTIANITY INTO THE PHILIPPINES

FIGURE 1

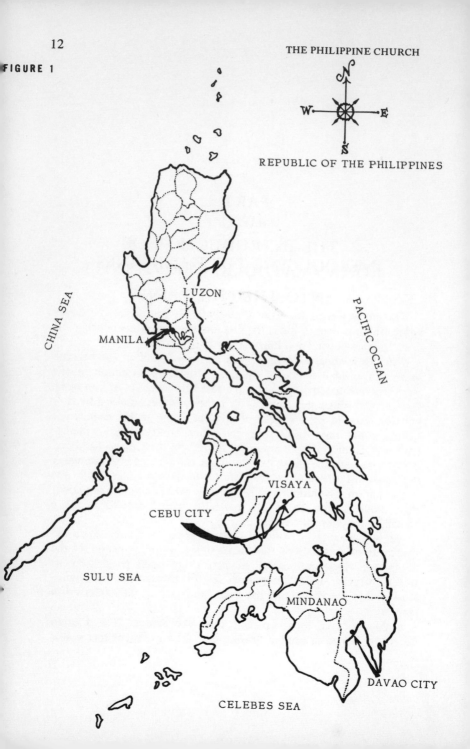

THE PHILIPPINE CHURCH

REPUBLIC OF THE PHILIPPINES

CHINA SEA

PACIFIC OCEAN

LUZON

MANILA

VISAYA

CEBU CITY

SULU SEA

MINDANAO

DAVAO CITY

CELEBES SEA

CHAPTER 1

INTRODUCING THE PHILIPPINES

The hostess slaps the side of the bus. At this signal the driver swings the bus over to the curb. You join the passengers pouring out — or "getting down," as a Filipino would express it.

"So this is Quiapo, Manila!" you say to yourself as you become immersed in what is one of the most crowded intersections in the world: an estimated 400,000 people pass here in a day. As you work your way through the crowd — or rather are carried along by it — you are assailed by a variety of vendors, some selling sweepstake tickets, some Juicy Fruit gum, and others selling religious medallions and candles. People are lined up outside the Quiapo cathedral in order to seek the blessing of the Black Nazarene, the image which has made this cathedral so important to the devout Roman Catholics of this nation. The humid heat of the day makes you more impatient than usual as you shake off a vendor who has tried to pin a medallion on your shirt as you pass by.

As you make your way up Quezon Boulevard, you notice the multitude of small shops that make it the shopping center of the Philippines. Transistor radios sunglasses, ball-point pens, kerosene stoves, bicycles and teteron material for trousers all say unmistakably that the Philippines has been caught up in the modern rush for things.

Suddenly you look up and read the words "Far Eastern University." You remember hearing that the enrollment this year is

60,000. Could this be the largest university in the world? What is it doing down here in this part of the world which is Quiapo? Walking past the school you can hear the sounds of crowded buildings — sounds of thousands of young people being educated in what must be described as an educational factory.

The crowds, the religion, the students — this is the Philippines today. Living in this little world, I as a Christian missionary have had to face the question: Do we in the evangelical Christian Church have a Word today for this young, vigorous and rapidly growing nation that is so desperately seeking its national identity and destiny? I believe most emphatically that we do have this needed Word. This Word is the Gospel — the Good News about the Lord Jesus Christ, the Divine Son of God who so deeply loves the vast multitudes of this and every nation.

But being deeply concerned about the communication of this Good News, I have had to ask a further question: How can the Gospel be most effectively presented in this dynamic society so that the Church of the Lord Jesus Christ can experience maximum growth, both in numbers and in quality? In seeking the answer, I have come to realize the truth of a very important principle of church growth: that the Church grows in a specific context, a specific matrix which is the society itself. Hence the emphasis upon sociology in this book. I am deeply convinced that to achieve maximum growth in the Philippines today, the Church must first understand the society in which it is growing. Evangelistic strategies must be formulated in the light of this precise knowledge. As intelligence regarding the enemy is of utmost importance in formulating strategy in wartime, so the more we can know of the people, the more effective our total witness will be, especially in the cross-cultural situation. Evangelistic witness demands a deep involvement in the lives of those to whom we are bringing the message. We need to know their psychological make-up, their patterns of relationship with one another, their entire social environment. In this way we can actually communicate *with* people, not *at* them.

Culturally and historically the Philippines is a unique nation. No other nation in Asia has experienced the same cultural transformations. The nation began as a loose grouping of Malayan tribes. These were suddenly swept into the Western orbit by the Spanish. Following this the society underwent a partial Americanization, and now it finds itself making its own way as a sovereign state in the Southeast Asian family of nations.

Studying these cultural transitions, I was struck by the fact that they occurred during definite historical crises and also that it was during these crises that tremendous religious changes took place. Seeing this helped me to formulate a second basic principle of church growth. That is, that the great advances of the Church have not occurred at just any time, regardless of the historical, cultural and social environment, but have happened at special, opportune times. The concept of the opportune time is so important that the Greeks had a special word for it: *kairos*. This word was used in contrast to *chronos*, which referred to clock and calendar time. We should not allow our theological distinctions between salvation history and ordinary history to prevent our seeing the hand of God moving in all of history, even today.

As if in miniature, the story of Christianity in the Philippines is an illustration of this "kaironic" nature of the growth of the Church. It is a series of advances at opportune moments in history, and the advances were very much influenced by the social environment. In this book we will note especially these historical and sociological factors. These will not "explain" the growth, but they will illustrate the way the Church actually grows in history and in its environment.

The Philippines has experienced three great historical periods of crisis: The Spanish conquest, the American acquisition, and Philippine attainment of independence. We will attempt to describe the historical forces at work in each of these periods. But this is not intended to be a book on history, as it is not a book on sociology. Its focus is the dynamics of the growth of the Christian Church in the Philippines. As we consider the historical and sociological aspects of this story, then, we will constantly need to ask ourselves, What does this mean for the growth of the Church? How did the timing of the entrance of Spain into the Philippines help or hinder the growth of Christianity in the islands? Or — What do the changes going on today in the structure of the modern Filipino family mean for effective evangelistic strategy? These are the kinds of questions that we must ask as we make this broad survey of the growth of the Church in the Philippines.

But before proceeding to our investigation, we want to introduce the Philippines a little more formally, especially for readers who may not be very familiar with this country.

THE LAND

Off the southeastern coast of China, between Taiwan and Borneo, lies the beautiful archipelago of tropical islands which is today the home of the vigorous young nation known as the Republic of the Philippines. This compact group of 7,000 islands, only 463 of which have areas of at least one square mile, has a total area of 115,600 square miles — a little larger than the State of Arizona. Luzon in the north is its largest and most heavily populated island. Mindanao in the south is the second largest island and today represents the frontier, as it is still relatively underpopulated. Between the two is an important group of islands collectively known as the Visayan Islands. The mountainous character of much of the islands gives the general impression of a rugged topography. There are several plains, notably the central plains of Luzon, in which most of the agricultural production takes place.

THE CLIMATE

Insular and located within the tropics, the Philippines has a climate which is "basically maritime and tropical. It is characterized by uniformly high humidity, abundant rainfall, continuous heat" (Eggan 1956:17). Some Westerners find the climate pleasant, but others are quite uncomfortable in the humid heat. The Philippines experiences a remarkably equable climate, with the temperatures in the lowlands very seldom dipping below 65 degrees in the early morning or rising above 95 degrees in the afternoon. Cooler temperatures prevail in the higher altitudes. The two major seasons are the rainy and the dry, and it is in the length and intensity of the rainy season that we see the most regional variation. This particular variation in climate is an important factor in the agriculture of the various regions.

THE PEOPLE AND THEIR CULTURE

The people of the Philippines are racially of Malayan origin, but with quite an admixture of Chinese and European blood. The only exception is the Negrito group, which represents a vanishing minority. Although they have formed a surprisingly viable nation, the people are fragmented geographically, linguistically and, to some extent, religiously. There are about eight major language groups, of which Cebuano and Tagalog are the largest, and eighty or more minor language groups. The religion of the country is divided among the Moros, Christians and Pagans. The Moros are the Moslem peoples of Mindanao and Sulu. The Pagans are the predominantly animistic mountain groups. The Christians make up the majority of the population (about 90 per cent). In mid-1968 the total population stood at 35,900,000, growing at a rate of 3.5 per cent per year.

The culture, as we shall see more in detail later, is an interesting blend of Orient and Occident. It is probably the most Western of any oriental society. In his book, *The Hispanization of the Philippines* (1959), Phelan draws our attention to three buildings which we can see in any town in the Philippines. First is the nipa palm house built up off the ground, the typical home of the *barrio*. In the center of town is the Roman Catholic church or cathedral. The third building is the schoolhouse. According to Phelan, these three symbolize the three cultural strands which have intertwined to form the culture of modern Philippines: the Malayan, Spanish and American. Each has made its own distinctive contribution to the enrichment of this unique society.

Helpful as it is, Phelan's thumbnail description of Philippine culture leaves us a little uneasy. Modern Philippines is not simply a bland combination of Malayan, Spanish and American cultures. It is a living, growing thing and exhibits a dynamic uniqueness all its own that can be described only as modern Filipino.

This distinctive character of modern Filipino culture has become increasingly evident since Independence. The postwar period of crisis during which this culture is being developed is not yet over. The twenty-four years since Independence would be only a very short period in the history of any nation. The Philippines is forming its character as an independent Southeast Asian country in a world severely troubled by ideological and nationalist struggles. It is also beset by severe internal problems which are aggravated by continued social unrest and a skyrocketing population growth. Sabah, Vietnam, Huk raids, along with stories of crime and politics, crowd the pages of the Manila daily newspapers.

The Philippines is also in crisis in regard to religious affairs. The nationalistic and nativistic sects, many of which have arisen since the war, continue to grow. Protestant Christianity is experiencing a radically changing scene, particularly due to the entrance of many postwar missions. The Catholic Church has begun to feel the effects of Vatican II. As we have already noted, this is the third period of crisis through which the Philippines has passed. For perspective to help us navigate these turbulent seas of crisis, we need to turn back the pages of history and study how the Christian Church has fared in the other critical periods.

The prospects for growth of Evangelical Christianity are promising, but the strategies to achieve this growth still await formulation. The task of this book is to provide some needed background in order that effective strategies may be developed for the greater growth of Christ's Church.

CHAPTER 2

ROMAN CATHOLIC CHRISTIANITY ARRIVES IN THE PHILIPPINES

The story of the growth of Christianity in the Philippines began with the arrival of Roman Catholic Christianity during Magellan's visit to the islands in 1521. To help us understand how cultural and historical factors influenced the pattern of the growth of the Christian religion at that time, we will re-create, as far as our sources allow, the state of Philippine society and religion at the time of the arrival of the first Europeans in the sixteenth century. Who were the people who inhabited the islands then? What was their history? their religion? their social structure? In seeking the answers to these questions we immediately face the problem of what is called "pre-history." Some may even say that in this early period we are actually out of the realm of history and in the realm of pure conjecture. However, the picture may be not quite that dark.

The grand old man of Philippine archeology and anthropology, Dr. H. Otley Beyer, has given us a helpful outline of Philippine history which will serve as the framework for our historical investigations. He divides Philippine history into three broad periods. First is the Prehistoric Period, from the arrival of the first men to about the beginning of the Christian era. Archeology is the only source of firm information concerning this period. The second is the Protohistoric Period, from the beginning of the Christian Era until the arrival of Magellan in 1521. The sources for this period are archeological findings and scattered historical references to the Philippines in the records of nearby countries such as China. The third period is the

Historic Period, dating from the arrival of Magellan until the present. Here the written records are almost continuous, and we are on firm historical ground (Beyer and de Veyra 1947:1).

We shall give most of our attention to the Historic Period, for only here do we have history as it is generally conceived. But to understand the actual state of the Philippines when the Spaniards arrived, we shall briefly survey what is known of the earlier period. For the Philippines was not a *carte blanche* on which Spain could simply impress a pure European culture and religion. To appreciate the uniqueness of the Philippines today as an unusual blend of the Orient and Occident, we must understand something of the early history of the people.

PRE-SPANISH HISTORY AND RELIGION

As we begin to unravel the cultural history of the early Filipino, we immediately enter a large area of current debate in modern anthropology concerning the racial origins of the Filipino and the theories of prehistoric migrations. The widely quoted conclusions of Dr. Beyer concerning the six or seven distinct migrations into the Philippine Islands from the surrounding areas are now being disputed by more recent investigators.[*]

In the development of his theory, Beyer identified the different migration groups with various groups in the living populations. It is here that his theories have been most open to attack. Modern investigators, such as Keesing and Fox, feel that the racial pool has been so well mixed that to separate the various types at this late date is impossible. Even Kroeber, who accepted the basic distinctions in racial types, records several items of contradictory evidence. He says, for example, that "so far as language relationships are concerned, geographical position and not adherence to a particular racial type is clearly the determining factor" (1928:76). Likewise he registers surprise at finding the Malayan-type fire piston among the "Indonesian" interior peoples.

Recently Keesing has brought forward the possibility that the famous Ifugao terracing system may have developed as late as the beginning of Spanish times and thus challenges the migration theory at a very sensitive point. Fox feels that Beyer's view is an

[*] A list of these seven supposed migrations may be found in Eggan 1956:253-256.

"oversimplification which does not allow for the possibility of variant developments in local response to types of land use, residence patterns, ecological setting, and so forth" (Eggan 1956:257).

Fortunately for the purposes of our investigation, we do not need to enter into this very interesting debate at any great length. Some important facts about Philippine origins seem to be quite clear. One is that when the Spaniards arrived in the sixteenth century, the islands were inhabited by at least two distinctly different types of peoples: the Negrito and the Malayan.

The Negritos were a small minority found mainly in the remote mountain regions. These people, called *Aeta* by the Tagalogs, are a negroid pigmy people, nomadic food gatherers and hunters of simple culture who are treated with disdain by the more highly civilized Malayan groups. They must have arrived in very early times, possibly traveling across then-existing land bridges connecting Borneo and the Philippines. Their language has been lost (what are now listed as Negrito languages are only dialectical variations of the languages of the nearby Malayan group) and their culture has been so modified by contact with other groups that their own primeval culture and beliefs cannot be reconstructed (Kroeber 1928:19).

All of the other groups, diverse as they may be, are racially what has been termed "Southern Mongoloid" (*Kayumanggi* in Tagalog), and recognize their basic racial unity. Many of these were seafaring peoples and as such probably arrived in the Philippines in boats at various times. Some of these Malayan tribes, possibly the earlier ones, settled in or were driven into the mountain areas and became quite hostile toward outsiders. Some engaged in headhunting and were both feared and looked down upon by the lowlanders. There were thus probably many waves of migrations from different parts of Southeast Asia. Borneo, Java, Indochina and South China represent several probable points of origin.

As the islands were being populated, a series of related societies emerged, especially along the coastal and river valley areas. These societies, like their languages, were quite diverse in many respects, yet showed many underlying common patterns. These common patterns point to a natural affinity in the great Malayo-Indonesian culture area. They include certain important social structures which we will consider in some detail in the next chapter.

Malayan Migrations Bring Animism

In religion we also find common patterns which point to a common animistic religious heritage of all these peoples. Much of this basic animistic belief structure persists even to the present day and must be taken into account in all evangelistic preaching, whether in the lowlands or in the mountain areas.

A Spanish student of Tagalog religion in the last century summarized the ancient religion of the Tagalogs in this way: "It consisted in the worship (*culto*) of invisible beings called *anitos*. They believed in the *Nono,* which represented the spirits of the ancestors, and had priestesses called *babaylanas*" (Lopez 1894:38). This basic framework would apply to all early Philippine religion, although the terminology would vary somewhat from region to region. The fundamental concept is that of the *anito*. Concerning this term Kroeber says:

> This term is hard to translate, because it includes gods or divinities proper, evil or beneficent spirits of lower rank; and finally the souls of dead human beings. An *anito* is therefore any being which possesses the intelligence of a human person and equal or superior facilities, but lacks corporeal body. The word is of widespread use in the East Indies and Oceania, and the concept of *anito* is undoubtedly an extremely ancient one in this part of the world. Its particular meaning varies somewhat from tribe to tribe in the Philippines, some groups thinking rather of gods and spirits, and others primarily of the souls of dead human beings, when they use the term (1928:187).

The basically animistic character of primitive Philippine religion is clear. The cult was not highly developed. Legaspi reported that "there are not known among them either the temples or the rites and ceremonies of other people" (Blair, Robertson 1903:Vol. II, 235). The religious practitioners were women shamans, called *babailanes* in Visayan or *katalonanes* in Tagalog, who were called in to make sacrifices. Often these sacrifices were for healing. On these occasions feasts called *manganitos* were often held (Blair, Robertson 1903:Vol. III, 164). Many features of this primitive religion have proven very tenacious and are still found in all sections of the country. Among the so-called pagan mountain groups the ancestral faith continues today with very little change.

Indian and Chinese Influences in Pre-Spanish Times

When the Spaniards arrived, in the sixteenth century, they did not find a country completely untouched by outside civilizations. Magellan had not been the first foreigner to set foot on Philippine soil, although he may have been the first European. We should not therefore speak of the "discovery of the Philippines" by Magellan, but rather of his "arrival."

The first foreign contact probably was that of Indian traders, possibly as early as the second century. In the seventh century the Sri-Vishaya Empire, of Buddhist orientation, rose in southeastern Borneo. This empire, expanding until about the twelfth century, eventually dominated the major island of western Indonesia, the Malay Peninsula, and possibly the Philippines and the southern part of Formosa. It may have been from this empire that the central islands of the Philippines received their name, the Visayan (or Bisayan) Islands.

In the thirteenth century, the Sri-Vishayan Empire was destroyed by the rising Javanese Madjapahit Empire. This empire was Brahmanistic in character and for over a century exerted its influence upon Philippine life and religion. Religious artifacts from this period have been recovered and testify to the Hinduistic character of this influence.

The impress of Indian civilization upon protohistoric Philippines can be seen especially in the areas of language and religion. Tagalog and other Philippine languages have many words of Indian or Sanskrit origin, for example, and possibly significantly, *guro* (meaning teacher). At the time of the arrival of Spain in the islands, seventeen tribes were literate, as some among them knew how to read and write according to an ancient syllabary of Indic origin (Eggan 1956:260). Hindu religious ideas can be seen in the religious vocabulary of the people as well as by the presence of Hindu images. According to Blumentritt, *Bathala,* the Tagalog word for the Supreme Being, "comes from *Batara-guru,* a name which is given to Siva, one of the three gods (Brahma, Siva and Vishnu) that form the *trimurti* or trinity of the Hindus. Bhattara signifies *lord* in Sanskrit (1948:235)." Kroeber warns us, however, against picturing Hinduism as coming into the Philippines as an organized religion (1918:46), although the witness of an early Chinese trader to a *suttee* (widow burning in the funeral pyre of her husband) may be evidence of a rather substantial Hindu cult in the Tagalog area.

Over the centuries the Chinese (and to a much lesser extent, the Japanese) had enjoyed a brisk trade with the islands. They apparently came to know of them through Arab traders in about the ninth century. By the thirteenth century they dominated trade with the Philippines, their junks following a definite circular route around Southeast Asia. For a while Chinese interest, or power, seemed to drop off, but again in the fifteenth century, just before the trade-seeking ships from the West arrived, the Chinese made another attempt to dominate the entire region through trade under the second Ming emperor, Yung Lo. Thus when the Spanish arrived they found Chinese vessels trading, especially in and about Luzon and Mindoro.

Chinese influence was greater in the area of material culture than in religion or social structure. This might be expected from the Chinese with their strictly businesslike interest in trade. Cottons, silks, iron and tin products constituted much of the wares which the Chinese brought in exchange for gold, waxes and cinnamon. Their jars became especially prized as heirlooms by many of the islanders.

Summing up these two strands of influence, Kroeber says:

> It is true that the influences of the Chinese have been those of traders, the less direct but more profound influences of the Hindus those of teachers. But in both cases the influences penetrated as isolated bits, not as compact systems (1918:50).

The Coming of Islam

The last of the major pre-Spanish influences to reach the Philippines was that of Islam. In its march eastward Islam had become securely established in India by A.D. 1200. About the middle of the fourteenth century an Arabian scholar, Makdum, reached the Moluccas. He then moved into the Mindanao-Sulu area and began to propagate the Moslem faith there in about 1380. A Rajah Baginda from Sumatra arrived, followed by a very important Moslem leader, Abu Bakr, who settled in Sulu in 1450 — only seventy years before Magellan arrived. Abu Bakr married a daughter of Rajah Baginda and declared himself sultan of the area, thus establishing the first Moslem sultanate in Sulu at the southern tip of the Philippines.

Thus began the growth of Islam in the Philippines. Its influence in the South was profound. It introduced a new religion, a new government and a new learning. Its influence spread and was beginning to make advances in Luzon, especially around Manila, when the Spanish arrived there. An early (1609) Spanish historian, Morga, stated that natives of Borneo trading and intermarrying in the Manila-Tondo area were responsible for introducing Islam there (Blair, Robertson 1903:Vol. XVI, 134). The hold of Islam on these peoples in the North was as yet very weak. The people knew of circumcision, and of the prohibition on eating pork, but had absorbed very little else of the Prophet's teachings.

It might be termed ironic that Spain, which had just checked the western expansion of Islam within her own borders, would find herself meeting the same religion head-on in its farthest eastern extension. This fact could not help but reinforce their conviction of the holy nature of their mission to bring this part of the world into subjection to the True Faith. Indeed, for all Christians there was surely something providential in this whole historical development.

This, then, was the Philippines at the time of the arrival of the Spanish: a cluster of Malayan cultures and peoples, basically animistic in religion, though somewhat influenced in varying degrees by Hinduism, with a recent incursion of Islam. We turn now to the story of the entrance of Roman Catholic Christianity into the Philippines through the Spanish conquest.

THE SPANISH CONQUEST

The Arrival of Magellan

At the beginning of the sixteenth century the two small Iberian countries, Spain and Portugal, were at work carving up the world between them. To lessen conflict, Pope Alexander VI exercised his worldwide powers by drawing the Demarcation Line in 1493, neatly splitting the new world in two: half for Spain, half for Portugal. It was during this period of Iberian expansion that a Portuguese explorer-adventurer, Ferdinand Magellan, became interested in finding a westward route to the Spice Islands (the Moluccas). He had previously been in Malacca, and there had acquired a Malayan slave. His king, however, was not interested. Magellan moved to Spain and found there a more favorable response from King Charles I. A small fleet of five ships was outfitted and set sail on September 20, 1519. The voyage was plagued with troubles, including a mutiny. It was with only three ships that Magellan crossed the Pacific after passing through the straits which now bear his name. On March 16, 1521, he sighted Samar Island in the Philippines. The following day he landed on a small, uninhabited island of Homonhon, near Leyte, the first landing of a European on Philippine soil. Moving on to the island of Limasawa, Magellan met his first Philippine chiefs (whom he called "kings"). There on Easter Sunday, March 31, 1521, a mass was held, and Magellan laid claim to the islands in the name of the King of Spain, naming them the "Archipelago of St. Lazaro."

Leaving Limasawa, he sailed to the more important island of Cebu, arriving there on April 7. On the same day he entered into a friendly blood compact with Rajah Humabon. This rather impressive ceremony was performed by each leader drawing some blood from his arm and mixing it in a cup of wine. Each then drank from the cup, sealing the pact of friendship. In port at the same time was a Siamese trader, indicating that Cebu was not unaccustomed to contacts with the outside world.

The first baptisms occurred at this time. Pigafetta, the official chronicler of the expedition, reports that the queen and eight hundred others were baptized (Blair, Robertson 1903:Vol. XXXIII, 159). Another writer, Maximilianus Transylvanus, reported in 1523 that the chief and 2,200 "Indians" were baptized (Blair, Robertson 1903:Vol. I, 323). It is an interesting question as to how much of the Christian faith these converts either understood or received. Although his figures may not be as reliable as those of Pigafetta, Transylvanus does add an interesting detail which may give us a clue as to the reason for the quick acceptance of baptism. It seems that the chief's nephew had been sick for two years. He was told to devote himself to Christ and he would regain his former health. He consented and adored the cross, received baptism and the next day declared he was well again (Blair, Robertson 1903:Vol. I, 323). This was not to be the last time that a magical healing efficacy would be attributed to baptism.

Magellan's visit, which had begun so auspiciously, came quickly to a tragic end. Chief Lapu-Lapu of Mactan, a small neighboring island, had a quarrel with Humabon. Magellan, wanting to encourage Humabon as a "Christian" sovereign to rule over the islands, and incidentally to demonstrate the power of Spanish arms, decided to intervene. Taking with him forty men, he was met by a force of 3,000 (according to Transylvanus). The small Spanish force was defeated and Magellan was slain on April 26, 1521 (Blair, Robertson 1903:Vol. I, 323). By involving himself in a local dispute, Magellan tragically gave up his opportunity to complete his circumnavigation of the world. In fact, the entire expedition was threatened, as the Cebuanos apparently lost what little Christianity they had and massacred twenty-seven Spaniards. The survivors escaped to the Moluccas. There they picked up a load of spices and returned to Spain. They arrived on September 6, 1522, with only one ship and eighteen survivors. It was an epic achievement gained at great cost. The Philippines had been found. It only remained to seize them permanently.

The rivalry between Portugal and Spain over the Moluccas and the Philippines became more intense as Spain continued to send expeditions to these islands. The Treaty of Zaragoza (1529) settled the question as far as the Moluccas were concerned: They were Portugal's. The status of the Philippines was not so clear. Spain continued to send expeditions. Villalobos, in his expedition of 1542, gave the islands their present name, naming them after Prince Philip (later to become Philip II) of Spain. No permanent Spanish settlement in the islands resulted from these early expeditions.

The Great Expedition of Legaspi

The story of the Spanish conquest of the Philippines properly begins with the expedition led by Miguel Lopez de Legaspi, a wealthy resident of Mexico City. The motivations behind this expedition were both commercial and missionary. The Spanish wanted to find a route from Mexico to the "Western Islands," and back to Mexico again, without passing through the Portuguese Moluccas. They were also under a strong religious compulsion to set the stage for a Christian conquest of pagan China and Japan. The islands were considered a vital stepping stone to the achievement of this goal.

On March 21, 1564, Legaspi set sail from Puerto de Navidad on the west coast of Mexico with two galleons and two smaller ships, under sealed orders — sealed because they included instructions involving the controversial entry into Portuguese-dominated waters. A vital part of this expedition was the complement of five Augustinian missionaries whose job it was to begin the work of Christianizing the population of the Philippines. Their leader was an experienced monk, Father Andres de Urdaneta, a relative of Legaspi. This was not Urdaneta's first visit to these parts. As a young man, before entering the priesthood, he had sailed with the ill-fated Loaisa Expedition of 1525. On the present voyage he served both as navigator and spiritual leader.

Legaspi arrived at Cebu on February 13, 1565, but decided against immediate landing because of the hostility of the people. He first explored several other islands, including Bohol, before returning to Cebu on April 27, 1565. This time he met force with superior force. The town was burned, and the petty king Tupas capitulated. On the site of the former town, Legaspi established the new Cebu City, which he devoutly named the "City of the Most Holy Name of Jesus." In spite of this use of force, Legaspi seems to have been genuinely committed to a minimum use of force to attain his objectives. Because of this policy the conquest of the Philippines contrasts sharply with that of Mexico and Peru, and intentionally so. The official policy was to support the incumbent chiefs militarily in return for recognition of Spanish sovereignty and payment of tribute. Because of this policy, Legaspi soon achieved friendly relations with Chief Tupas and the Cebuano people, whom the Spaniards called the *pintados,* or "painted ones," because of their tattooed bodies.

Meanwhile a usable though dangerous return route from the Philippines was found. The ships would sail northward and then eastward across the Pacific, then down the coast of California to Navidad, and from there to Acapulco, Mexico. Regular voyages began between Mexico and the Philippines, paving the way for the famed galleon trade of the seventeenth and eighteenth centuries. In 1568 reinforcements arrived for Legaspi. Among these was his grandson, Juan de Salcedo, who was soon to gain fame as 'the "Conqueror of Luzon."

In these early days in Cebu, Legaspi was frequently bothered by Portuguese interference. For this reason, in 1569 he transferred his headquarters to Iloilo, Panay Island. Here an expedition was formed of Spanish soldiers and Visayan natives. The master-of-camp (captain) was de Goite, and Salcedo served as second in command of the force. Their first stop was Mindoro (called Vindoro in the early sources). Here they encountered some Chinese trading junks. The first landing in Luzon was made directly opposite Mindoro in Balayan in what is now the province of Batangas. They made a short trip up to beautiful Lake Taal and then proceeded by ship to Manila.

Manila at this time was a town of about 2.000 inhabitants, ruled by a Moslem, Rajah Soliman. Directly across the Pasig River was another settlement in what is now Tondo. This was ruled by Soliman's uncle, Rajah Lakandula. For some reason the old man Lakandula was quite friendly to the Spaniards, but his nephew was not, although he did appear so at first. After making a blood compact, Soliman and his Moros treacherously attacked the Spaniards. In retaliation the Spaniards burned down Manila. The force then returned, this time under the personal command of Legaspi. Soliman withdrew his forces from Manila, regrouped in the north and then returned to attack the Spaniards from the sea. Soliman was killed in this battle, and Legaspi firmly established Spanish authority in the area. On June 24, 1571, Legaspi proclaimed Manila a Spanish city and moved his headquarters there. Only a year later Legaspi died, on August 20, 1572.

Reading over his correspondence and reports, one is impressed by the ability and dedication of this man. This venture cost him his wealth, but gained him an important niche in the history of Spain and of the Philippines. One does not have to approve of the Spanish imperialism of that day to recognize and appreciate the great civilizing force which Legaspi unleashed on the Philippines.

The actual extension of Spanish rule over all of Luzon was carried out primarily by Legaspi's grandson, Salcedo. Salcedo has been compared with Cortes of Mexico, but the comparison may not be especially helpful in view of the difference in methods used by the two men. Salcedo subdued the different areas by an astute use of minimum force and diplomacy. There were, however, some sharp battles. The taking of Cainta near Manila resulted in the destruction of the town and the killing of a large portion of the population. But this was the exception. The number of soldiers used, for example, when Salcedo took the northern Ilocos area was only forty-five. In some cases, Visayan *pintados* fought alongside the Spaniards. Modern Philippines historians are probably reading in too much of the modern nationalistic attitude when they speak of the early *datus* (chiefs) fighting against the Spanish in order to preserve "Philippine liberty." It was rather a few groups, more or less disunited, resisting Spanish domination.

Salcedo died at the early age of twenty-seven, on March 11, 1576. At the time of his death the conquest of the Philippines was militarily effectively completed. The only areas which remained out of Spanish control were the Moslem areas of Mindanao and Sulu and the interior tribes in the mountainous areas, particularly in northern Luzon.

Roman Catholic missionary work began immediately upon the arrival of Legaspi in 1565. Morga (1609) comments:

> From the earliest beginning of the conquest and pacification of the Filipinas Islands, the preaching of the holy gospel therein and the conversion of the natives to our holy Catholic faith was undertaken. The first to set hand to this task were the religious of the Order of St. Augustine, who went there with the adelantado Legaspi in the fleet of discovery, and those of the same order who went afterward to labor in this work, and toiled therein with great fervor and zeal. Thus, finding the harvest in good season, they gathered the first fruits of it, and converted and baptized many infidels throughout the said islands (Blair, Robertson 1903:Vol. XVI, 150).

Before we proceed to study further how Roman Catholic Christianity actually spread among the peoples of the islands, we will first take a closer look at the people among whom it spread. What was their culture? What was their social structure? family structure? What kind of political organization did they have? What was the structure of their social classes? After answering these questions we will be better able to understand the actual process of the religious and social change usually referred to as the Christianization of the Philippines.

CHAPTER 3

SIXTEENTH CENTURY
PHILIPPINE SOCIETY

"Where I fell down, there I will rise" is the translation of a Tagalog saying meaning that the faith of my fathers will be my faith also. Tradition is a strong social control in any society, especially in those societies which have a strong family base. That the society and culture of a people affect the growth of the Church among that people is axiomatic in church growth studies.

Why this is so is not hard to understand. From the early days of the New Testament Church, social and cultural factors as well as religious factors have greatly influenced the growth of the Church among specific peoples. That many priests believed in the early Jewish Church (Acts 6:7), while the philosophers at Athens proved unresponsive (Acts 17:32), points to social and cultural factors as well as religious. Similarly, the resistance of the tight social organization of sixteenth century Japanese society to the entrance of the Christian faith stands in sharp contrast to the more or less ready acceptance of Roman Catholic Christianity by the much more fragmented and less highly developed Philippine society of the same period. But before generalizing concerning sixteenth century Philippine society, we should pause to examine it in greater detail.

GENERAL DESCRIPTION

For a description of the culture and society of the early Filipinos we are almost completely dependent upon the writings of their conquerors. Pre-Spanish Philippine records are practically non-

31

existent, but a few valuable early documents have been found. The first description of the early Philippines which we have is found in the Chinese document *Chu-Fan-Chi* by Chao-Ju-Kua, written in about 1225:

> The country of Ma-it is north of Borneo, with over a thousand families settled together along both banks of a creek (or gully). The natives cover themselves with a sheet of cotton cloth, or hide the lower part of the body with a sarong.

> There are bronze images of gods of unknown origin scattered about in the grassy wilderness (Felix 1966:266).

Note especially the reference to the settlement pattern. We shall find similar references in later sources.

The Spanish conqueror Legaspi gives us his impressions of the islands and their peoples. In a letter dated July 23, 1567, he says that many islands were being discovered which were inhabited by many people, and that he did not anticipate much difficulty in converting them to Christianity

> because there are not known among them either the temples or the rites and ceremonies of other people, although they are a people extremely vicious, fickle, untruthful, and full of other superstitions. They all have many specimens of gold, and this they trade and wear as jewelry; but there is only a small quantity of it, by reason of there being no headmen or great lords among them (Blair, Robertson 1903:Vol. II, 235).

Then about a year later (June 26, 1568) he writes:

> The country is healthful and has a fair climate although it is very rough and mountainous. All trade therefore is by sea, and almost all the natives live on the seacoast and along the rivers and creeks that empty into the sea. In the interior there are few settlements, although in some islands there are blacks living in the mountains, who neither share nor enjoy the sea, but are most of the time at war with the Indians who live down on the sea-coast. Captives are made on both sides, and so there are some black slaves among the Indians (Blair, Robertson 1903:Vol. II, 241).

In this last letter, Legaspi refers to the "blacks," the people today known as the Negritos, who lived in the mountains, in sharp contrast to the lowlanders or sea-peoples. As the Spanish moved on through the islands, they quickly became acquainted with the major tribes. At first they seemed to classify the people broadly into four groups. First were the *pintados* (Visayan tattooed people), then the so-called *moros* (Tagalogs) of the Manila area. They soon found out about the Malayan mountain tribes who were to be distinguished from the Negritos. These were referred to by Governor Sande (1576) as the *"Tingguians,"* derived, he said, from the native word for "mountain." He compares them to the *chichimecos* (wild tribes) of Mexico (Blair, Robertson 1903:Vol. IV, 66). Finally, there were the Negritos to which Legaspi refers. As the Spanish became better acquainted with the peoples of the islands they began to add to this list such groups as the *ylocos* (Ilocanos). They quickly recognized a basic similarity between the lowland groups, and as they became Christianized they were simply referred to as *"indios"* (Indians). When the Tagalogs became Christian the word *moro* came to be used only for the Moslem peoples of the Sulu-Mindanao area.

Was this lumping together of the lowlanders a gross oversimplification? Or was there actually a cultural similarity between these peoples and tribes, significant enough for us to speak meaningfully of a generalized "lowland Philippine" society, or even of a "pan-Philippine" society? At this point we need to remind ourselves of the actual settlement patterns of the rather sparse population of sixteenth century Philippines. No great concentrations of people were to be found. Rather, the population was scattered throughout the many islands, divided in many ways. The simple geographic realities of the Philippines — the great number of islands, high mountain barriers, jungles and rivers — tended to keep these groups separate from each other. As a result, the peoples of the different areas tended toward a certain isolationism in their development which is reflected linguistically in the many languages and dialects of the Philippines.

But having said this, it must also be said that the lowland tribes and language groups had a remarkably similar social structure. So much so, in fact, that modern anthropologists such as Kroeber (1918), Fox (1955a) and Mednick (1965) say we are justified in generalizing and speaking of a pan-Philippine society. This question is of vital importance to our investigation, for if we can make valid generalizations concerning Philippine society as a whole, and especially concerning lowland Philippine society, then it will be much easier to make valid generalizations concerning the spread of Christianity in that society.

Working back from our knowledge of present-day Philippine society, both lowland and tribal, through the historical sources, Fox finds a series of cultural traits which he believes describe Philippine lowland society in the sixteenth century. These are summarized by Mednick as follows:

1. Community life and social activities organized on the basis of kinship and common economic and ritual interest.
2. Leadership and authority vested in the hands of family heads and mature and older persons . . . steeped in the wisdom of customary law who met together to settle disputes. Decisions made by consensus while participants involved are supported and defended by kinsmen.
3. Wealth distinctions, leading in some cases to the formation of amorphous and mobile social classes.
4. The elementary family the basic social, economic, and ritual unit, but with the network of primary relationships extended to consanguineal kin of both parents (i.e., the bilateral extended family).
5. Marriages arranged by go-betweens and involving protracted and elaborate gift-making.
6. Residence either patrilocal or matrilocal, or both alternately.
7. Divorce common until a child is born.
8. Jural equivalence of both sexes in regard to inheritance, ownership of property, with both sexes bringing their own property to a marriage and keeping it separate from their conjugal property.
9. Family and kindred responsibilities for vengeance.
10. Social distance between non-kindred bridged by patterns of reciprocal hospitality, generosity, and euphemistic speech.
11. Community defined in terms of blood-ties, marriage, ritual kinship, and these plus shared residence, common interests and experiences, added to community level ritual obligations, defined the community as a social rather than a political entity (1965:5).

It would seem that much of the above summary rests quite heavily upon recent descriptions of contemporary tribal societies. To test the validity of these generalizations for the early period under discussion we need to turn to an analysis of the documents of the period. Fortunately for us, some of the early Spanish arrivals were very interested in recording what they saw, so that their writings contain what could be termed the observations of amateur (but not armchair) anthropologists.

One source has been found particularly valuable. This is *Sucesos de Las Islas Philipinas* (Events of the Philippine Islands) by Antonio de Morga, often referred to simply as Morga's *Sucesos.* Morga was an official of the Spanish Colonial Government sent out from Mexico and stationed in Manila for a period of eight years. He then returned to Mexico in 1602 and there wrote this very complete early history which contains a valuable final chapter describing the islands and their people. The work was originally published in 1609, and we are fortunate to have it translated by Blair and Robertson and included in full in their famous work (1903). Philippine scholars such as Jose Rizal value this work highly for its basically sympathetic view of the Filipinos. Blair and Robertson include Rizal's helpful footnotes in their translation of *Sucesos* (Blair, Robertson 1903:Vol. XVI).

We shall look into these early documents to learn about the structure of the family, the political organization and the social classes of early Philippine society.

THE FAMILY AND KINSHIP STRUCTURE

The importance of the family in the study of how the Church grows in non-Western societies can hardly be over-stressed. Western society in recent times has tended to minimize the role of the family, but even there the family remains the primary social institution, and the Church neglects it to its own peril. Once it is understood that the Church grows within a social environment in ways that are profoundly influenced by this environment, the importance of understanding family structure is readily seen. The large group movements into Christianity which have been termed "people movements" by students of church growth, are basically family movements. That is, these movements grow along kinship lines. There are factors which make one of these movements different from another, but they all have this in common: the growth follows lines of kinship, and the actual pattern of growth in a particular movement will depend in part on the type of kinship structure involved. If we want to understand how the Church has grown in the Philippines, we must understand the family and kinship structure.

Looking back to the list of eleven basic characteristics of pan-Philippine society cited above, we notice that family or kinship structure is an important factor in nine out of the eleven. The statement (number four) that "the elementary family [is] the basic social, economic, and ritual unit" clearly indicates the fundamental importance of the family in Philippine life. This theme will run through our entire discussion.

Marriage in early Philippine society was generally monogamous, but concubinage may have been common. "They considered one woman, whom they married, as the legitimate wife and mistress of the house; and she was styled *ynasaba* [*asawa*]. Those women whom they kept besides her they considered as friends. The children of the first were regarded as legitimate and whole heirs of their parents" (Morga in Blair, Robertson 1903:Vol. XVI, 125).

Early Philippine marriage customs are described by both Morga (Blair, Robertson 1903:Vol. XVI, 124-126) and, in more detail, by Loarca (Blair, Robertson 1903:Vol. V, 153-161). According to Loarca, the ceremonies involved depended upon the social class of the persons concerned. When persons of the chief or *datu* class were married, the negotiations regarding the dowry, called in Tagalog the *bigay-kaya* (giving what one can), were carried out by a freeman acting as a go-between. The actual marriage ceremony involved a feast, and a simple ritual climaxed by a speech by an elder and the joining of hands over a dish of uncooked rice, which was then thrown over all attending the feast. Marriage among the commoners did not involve the ceremony of the joining of the hands over the dish of rice. For them, only a simple ceremony of drinking rice wine from a common cup was all that was necessary. The dowry depended upon the economic state of the individual, so the slaves married without dowry, and the poor slaves without ceremony. Divorce was easily gotten for the slightest cause. Since divorce involved property and dowry negotiations, the relatives of both parties examined and judged the case, with the older men acting as mediators.

An outstanding characteristic of the Philippine family, then and now, is its bilateral character. Kinship is reckoned through both husband and wife. The husband and wife in the Filipino family have always been remarkably equal in rights and authority. Some Catholic writers would like to attribute the high place of women in Philippine society to the influence of Christianity. This place, however, seems to have been built into the social structure long before the arrival of Christianity. The equality of man and woman is seen mythically in the story of the origin of the human race current among the Visayan tribes at the time of the arrival of the Spaniards and recorded by Loarca in 1583. The human race began, it was said, when the land breeze and the sea breeze were married and brought forth a reed (a shoot of bamboo?). When the reed grew it split into two sections; one became a man and was called Si Kalac, the other became a woman and was named Si Kabay, from which names the words *lalake* (man) and *babae* (woman) were derived (Blair, Robertson 1903:Vol. V, 121-123). It is significant that one term of reference for the wife in Tagalog is the *kabiyak* (fellow split) of the husband.

Students of social structure point out that the kinship terminology of a particular people reflects the more important relationships and distinctions of the social structure of that people (see Murdock 1960:77). In Appendix A we have described the present-day kinship terminology of the Tagalog people. We have not attempted to reconstruct the complete Tagalog kinship terminology of the sixteenth century since it seems quite likely that the main change has been the substitution of some Spanish terms for some of the original Tagalog terms, while the underlying structure has remained intact. A functional analysis should confirm what we have already said about Philippine family structure and point up other important features as well.

What important characteristics of Philippine social structure can then be observed in the Tagalog kinship terminology? First of all, we notice that the whole system is bilaterally symmetrical. That is, the relationships of a person traced through the family of his mother are terminologically equivalent to his relationships traced through the family of his father. Secondly, there is no distinction of sex in several important terms. Thus the term *kapatid* (sibling) refers to either brother or sister. To make a distinction a modifier (*na lalake* for boy or *na babae* for girl) must be added. *Anak* (child) and *apo* (grandchild) show the same characteristic, as do some other terms. This is consistent with the fact that in matters of property, inheritance and other rights, males and females have equal jural rights. We can thus confirm the statements made above concerning the bilateral character of the Filipino family.

Another feature observable in the kinship system is its generational character. The importance of this category is reflected in the respectful forms of speech in the Tagalog language. When addressing a person of an older generation one must use the respectful particle *po* in almost every sentence. (It should be noted that not all Philippine languages have this respectful form.) Generational respect is also shown by the custom of "kissing the hand" of the older relative by touching the hand of the relative to one's forehead. The difference of age even within one generation is important. A young Tagalog child, for example, must address his older brother as *kuya,* and an older sister as *ate.*

In a bilateral kinship system, kinship can be quite rapidly extended because it moves out equally on both the mother's and father's sides. The Tagalog recognizes cousins up to the seventh degree. These larger groupings are referred to as kindreds. Murdock says of the kindred:

> It is always Ego-oriented, i.e., composed of persons related to a particular individual (or group of siblings) bilaterally (literally "on both sides"). The members of a kindred, other than the core individual and his siblings, need not be, and frequently are not related to one another. In any society, kindreds necessarily overlap one another endlessly. They are not discrete units; a society can never be divided into separate kindreds as it can be segmented into discrete families, lineages, clans, or communities (1960:4).

Murdock goes on to point out that in societies characterized by this type of bilateral structure (called the "Eskimo" type) there is also an absence of any functionally important descent groups. Thus there are no clans. This seems to have been generally true in the Philippines, with the exception of the *datu* or chief class. There the datuship passed through the male line. Even here, however, wealth and physical prowess were important factors in maintaining the leadership in the community. As pointed out above, kindreds do not represent concrete sections of a community. Each person has his own kindred which overlaps with many others. This has great importance for political organization and also for church growth, as we shall see later.

We are dealing, then, with a society which can best be visualized as a complex system of many interlocking webs of family relationships which multiply with each generation. Any political organization based upon kinship therefore will likely be unstable and fragmented. Group movements, especially into the Church, will take place in relation to these webs of relationship. Even the rise of the elite will be shaped by the interlocking nature of these webs. It would thus be expected that as families acquired property and wealth of their own, descent and inheritance would become increasingly important. On the other hand, the bilateral pattern of inheritance would tend to make it difficult to acquire great possessions. The fact that Legaspi mentions that there were no great lords with large accumulations of wealth would indicate that our general analysis is fairly accurate.

Even today, this mosaic of kinship webs remains basic in Philippine society. Much of the fragmentary nature of Philippine political and religious life can be traced to this basic characteristic of the society. The internal life of the Church with its family factions reflects it. The fact that much of the growth of the Church follows family kinship web lines underlines the importance of this concept for the understanding of church growth in Philippine society.

Returning now to the earlier period, an important question remains. Were there any broader loyalties, beyond that of kinship? The people must have been conscious of tribal and language differences, but there appears never to have been any general tribal organization with chiefs and subchiefs ruling over large populations, as is common in Africa. Apparently one settlement could go to war against another settlement of the same language area as easily as against one of a different language area. Kinship, not tribal loyalty, seems to have been the great binding force in this early society.

POLITICAL ORGANIZATION

Before we examine the political organization of pre-Spanish Philippines, let us look first at the basic settlement pattern of the people. Corpuz describes the pattern and indicates its importance even today:

> The basic patterns of human settlement were set centuries ago: dwellings followed the lines of the coast or hugged the river banks. Today the lineal pattern persists and the traveler by aircraft observes elongated settlements of houses strung thinly along the roads and highways that were laid out in modern times (1965:7).

This basic pattern of settlement along the coasts and rivers is confirmed even by the early report (1225) of Chao-Ju-Kua (see page 32), and also by many of the early Spanish observers. It is seen even in the name of the Tagalog people. The word *tagalog* probably is derived from the phrase *"taga-ilog,"* which means "those from the river."

The total population of the Philippines at this early time is estimated to have been only about five or six hundred thousand. The major portion of this rather small population was fairly well scattered along the coast lines and major river valleys, with a few tribal groups isolating themselves in the mountain regions.

The many settlements which dotted the coasts of the islands were called *barangays.* This colorful term was first of all the name of one of their larger types of boats. Pigafetta mentions this boat as being used during Magellan's invasion of Mactan Island (Blair, Robertson 1903:Vol. XXXIII, 175). Were these settlements called *barangays* because their inhabitants were descended from a boatload of immigrants? This was the explanation given by the natives to the Spaniards concerning the origin of the term.

Much of the reliable information which we have concerning the *barangays* comes from Friar Juan de Plasencia, a Franciscan missionary in Laguna province from 1577 until his death in 1590. To obtain this information he says he

> collected Indians from different districts — old men, and those of most capacity, all known to me, and from them I have obtained the simple truth, after weeding out much foolishness, in regard to their government, administration of justice, inheritances, slaves and dowries (Blair, Robertson 1903:Vol. VII, 173).

Plasencia says that the people had chiefs called *datus,* "who governed them and were captains in their wars, and whom they obeyed and reverenced" (Blair, Robertson 1903:Vol. VII, 173). The *barangays* over which these *datus* ruled were usually 30 to 100 families in size and tended to congregate for mutual protection. They were not, however, subject to one another — "except in friendship and relationship." By this last term, Plasencia probably is referring to the kinship and marriage relationships that undoubtedly existed between nearby *barangays.* It would seem probable, in fact, that some of these *barangays* had come into existence by a process of "hiving off" the original *barangays.* This seems all the more likely as this tendency is characteristic of the bilateral kinship structure.

This brings us to an important question. Was there any "superbarangay" type of political organization? It is clear that there was no "Philippine nation" as such then, and some investigators, such as Kroeber, have denied that there was any development beyond the simple *barangay* type of government, except for a few unstable and passing confederations. However, the concept of confederation should not be treated lightly, as it seems to have become quite significant in pre-Spanish Philippines. The earliest Philippine document we have is a description of the confederation of Madyaas. This was written in ancient script on a banana leaf. It tells of a confederation of *barangays* on the island of Panay about the middle of the thirteenth century. It is also clear that when the Spaniards arrived in the sixteenth century they encountered rather large settlements of over two thousand families each in Sugbu (Cebu), Maynila (Manila) and Bigan (Vigan). Each of these was ruled by a *datu,* or rajah, whose authority was recognized over a fairly large area. Lapu-Lapu also led the not insignificant force of two or three thousand men on the island of Mactan against Magellan. Mednick makes the suggestion that "kings" such as Humabon of Cebu and Soliman of Manila were similar to the "port" kings which had arisen in Indonesia during this period (1965:12). Islam had already brought the sultanate to the Sulu region, and it seems clear that some types of larger governmental structures were beginning to be developed throughout the Philippines. The Spaniards arrived at a strategic time to bring the islands together with a central, though colonial, government. Thus the idea of a larger governmental structure might not have been as unwelcome as some have thought.

SOCIAL CLASSES

As it developed, the *barangay* society seems to have become quite feudalistic in character. Thus in each *barangay* were persons of several distinct social classes, each fulfilling a distinct role in the society. Many historians following Morga (Blair, Robertson 1903:Vol. XVI, 120-124) state that there were three social classes: the nobles (the *datu* and his relatives), the freemen (called *timaguas* or *timawas*) and the slaves (*alipins*), who were divided into two classes. We find, however, that Plasencia's description (Blair, Robertson 1903:Vol. VII, 174-179) differs slightly, but significantly, from Morga's. The highest class, according to Plasencia, was the chiefs (*datus*). Next were the nobles, called *maharlikas*. They did not pay tax or tribute to the *datu,* but were obligated to accompany him in war at their own expense. The third class were the commoners, or "first class" slaves, called *aliping namamahay* ("slave who lives in his own house"). These were free to marry and live in their own houses with their own property and gold, which would be inherited by their children. They served a *datu* or *maharlika* with half of their cultivated land. These, then, could be classified as serfs. The fourth class were the slaves who served their master in his house and on his cultivated lands. These were known as *mga aliping sa gigilid* and could be sold by their masters.

Some of the variation in the descriptions may be due to regional differences, but it seems that the main point of difference is, Who were the commoners? Other Spanish writers seem to have equated the *maharlika* and the *timawa,* but may not Plasencia have been correct in terming *maharlika* "nobles" and the first class slaves (or serfs) "commoners"? In present-day Tagalog *maharlika* has the connotation of highborn or noble. In any event, the two descriptions are in basic agreement in their description of the feudal character of early Philippine society.

This description has not been fully accepted by some modern anthropologists. They believe that the Spaniards were reading in too much of their own social structure at this point. Fox believes that these sharp class distinctions were present only in areas under Moslem influence and hence were a late development and not truly representative of Philippine society at that time (1955b:438). These distinctions may have been a late development and Islam certainly solidified the class distinctions. But it seems that all of Philippine lowland society was undergoing many changes during that period. To localize these developments in and around port communities such as Manila and Cebu may possibly be underestimating how really pervasive was the generalized lowland culture that we have been describing. The class terms were already well imbedded in the Tagalog, Ilocano and Visayan languages. It should also be noted that Plasencia wrote his account from the town of Nagcarlan, which though not too distant from Manila is remote enough to be considered rural Tagalog and not Manila culture. There is a tendency to describe early Philippine society in terms of present-day mountain tribal culture. This no doubt has some validity — the more, the farther back one goes. However, the record indicates that the lowland peoples were experiencing increasing outside contacts from the thirteenth century onward, and the changes going on in this period were probably considerable. There is, nevertheless, a valid warning in Fox's analysis against laying too much stress on the importance of the class structure as over against the very important underlying bilateral kinship structure with its leveling tendencies. The early Spanish observers probably were guilty of doing this.

The early Filipinos had both oral and written laws. Tradition was the primary social control in baranganic society. Interestingly, the legendary lawgiver was a woman, Lubluban, the great granddaughter of the first man and the first woman. Insult, murder, sorcery and the breaking of taboo were among the serious crimes. Often trial was by ordeal and debtors were sold into slavery.

Ruiz summarized the early political structure as follows:

> Within each baranganic political unit was found a governmental machinery under the direct control of a *datu* or chief. They had their own laws, written and unwritten; judicial procedures; and other social and political controls designed to maintain internal order and to promote the solidarity of the group. It is evident that this political unit was based chiefly on blood ties, and the in-group feeling and sentiment were so strong as to make external social and political relationships rather restricted. Any dealing with an out-group was primarily concerned with war or a question of marriage (1942:182).

This, then, was the shape of the society which Spain conquered and into which she introduced Christianity in the latter part of the sixteenth century. Tightly organized and highly structured on the local baranganic level, but quite fragmented and lacking cohesion beyond the local *barangay*, this society fell quickly and rather painlessly to the Spaniards. With the Spaniards came a new and aggressive religion, Roman Catholic Christianity.

We are now ready to tell the story of its entrance into the Philippines and its spread throughout the society which we have described.

CHAPTER 4

THE GROWTH OF ROMAN CATHOLIC CHRISTIANITY UNDER SPANISH RULE

Sailing across the Pacific in Legaspi's small fleet in 1565, Friar Andres de Urdaneta was busy at two tasks. As navigator of the expedition, he was plotting the course of the small ships towards the little-known islands of the Philippines. As leader of a small band of Augustinian monks, he was preparing for the beginning of missionary work among the people of those islands. In his dual role, Urdaneta illustrated the fact that the Spaniards never separated the expansion of their Empire from the spreading of their Faith. The two went hand in hand. Missions, in fact, came to serve as the justification for their imperialism. Many Spaniards were deeply conscious of the moral problems which their domination over distant people raised.

The Valladolid debate in 1550-1551, between Las Casas and Sepulveda, pointed up this concern. Las Casas was the reforming missionary-priest of the Americas, the "Champion of the Indians." Sepulveda was a classical scholar, a disciple of Aristotle. In this debate, Sepulveda answered Las Casas' charge of the illegitimacy of the conquest by pointing to the alleged injustices and tyrannies of the pre-Spanish regimes, and by asserting that some people were basically inferior to others and ought therefore to serve their betters (cf. Phelan 1959:25, Fagg 1963:211). Las Casas lost the debate, yet he deeply stirred the national conscience regarding the gross injustices perpetrated in the name of Christianity during the conquest of Latin America.

Thus in 1565, when Spain moved out to conquer the Philippines, the devout sovereign, King Philip II, was deeply concerned that the conquest and Christianization of the islands be carried out in accordance with Christian principles. He did not want a repetition of the Latin American experience. We have already seen in Chapter II how successful Legaspi and his grandson Salcedo were in conquering the islands and in introducing Christianity with a minimum use of force. We turn now to the story of the expansion of the Roman Catholic Faith in the Philippines. What were the reasons for this growth? Were the social factors important, and if so, how? We shall seek to understand and to evaluate critically, in the light of the records we have, exactly how the Spanish went about Christianizing the population; in other words, their missionary methods. The question will then follow: What are the lessons of this story for today's mission?

THE BEGINNINGS (1565-1576)

The five Augustinian missionary monks who accompanied Legaspi on his expedition under the leadership of Friar Urdaneta began the work of Christianizing the native population. We read of no great mass baptisms in these early days, in contrast to the visit of Magellan forty-four years earlier. During the first five years no more than one hundred were baptized. The force of Augustinians was slowly built up, but still in 1576 there were only thirteen friars, and their baptisms had been mostly of children (Phelan 1959:56).

Why this slow start? One reason, as Latourette and others point out, is that the attention of the early Spanish missionaries was fixed on China and Japan (Latourette 1939:Vol. 3, 309). They considered the Philippines a stepping stone to a greater prize. Another reason, possibly even more basic, was that the process of conquest, or "pacification," was still going on. The Spanish troops had to explore the various islands and bring their numerous *barangays* under Spanish sovereignty before the friars were really free to press forward in their mission work. Often a friar would accompany these expeditions, becoming himself an important factor in the pacification process.

The conquest was substantially complete by 1576, the year of the death of the young *"conquistador* of Luzon," Juan de Salcedo. The fact that the mission experienced a slow start during this period should not be taken to mean that nothing of significance had been accomplished. Languages were learned. Key conversions took place. The first baptism was that of an influential niece of the chief of Cebu, Rajah Tupas. This may have been related to her marriage during the same year to a member of Legaspi's expedition. Next came the conversion of a Moro who had served as an interpreter and was said to have had great influence. Then in 1568, three years after the arrival of Legaspi, Rajah Tupas himself, with his son, was baptized. "This opened the door to general conversion, for the example of Tupas had great weight" (Blair, Robertson 1903:Vol. I, 34). This also may have indicated their final acceptance of Spanish sovereignty. The political implications of the act would then have been as significant as the religious.

The dedication of these early missionaries is indicated by their immediate plunging into the study of the native languages. It is said that one, Friar Martin de Rada, was preaching in Visayan within five months. It was a slow beginning — but a great harvest was soon to be gathered.

THE GOLDEN AGE OF ROMAN CATHOLIC MISSIONS
(1576-1609)

The transition from conquest to colony was not smooth. The economic facts of life saw to this. The Philippines simply was not profitable to the colonizers. The pushing and pulling of conflicting interests were characteristic of this period. The settlers, friars, church officials and civil authorities were all involved — with the Filipinos in the middle. The process of Christianization, however, went on with great success. By the end of this brief period, the Roman Catholic Church had effectively established itself over the entire country, with the exception of the Moro-controlled regions of Mindanao and the tribal areas of northern Luzon. The process of Christianization was intimately related to the entire process of establishing Spanish civil rule in the colony. The missionary was, in fact, the personal extension of Spanish authority in his area. As Bourne comments:

> That it was the spirit of kindness, Christian love, and brotherly helpfulness of the missionaries that effected the real conquest of the islands is abundantly testified by qualified observers of various nationalities and periods, but the most convincing demonstration is the ridiculously small military force that was

required to support the prestige of the Catholic king. The standing army organized in 1590 for the defense of the country numbered four hundred men. No wonder an old viceroy of New Spain was wont to say: "En cada fraile tenía el rey en las Filipinas un capitan general y un ejercito entero" — "In each friar in the Philippines the king had a captain-general and a whole army" (Blair, Robertson 1903:Vol. I, 41-42).

Bourne may have underestimated the effectiveness of the "ridiculously small military force" with guns and ships in the primitive, fragmented society of early Philippines, but the above does seem to be the judgment of history on the effectiveness of the early missionaries as colonial agents. Surely they stand in great contrast to the rapacious traders and soldiers of other areas and times.

As missionaries, the friars worked within the context of the Spanish colonial policies. They were agents of the State as well as servants of the Church. An understanding of these colonial policies, then, is necessary for an understanding of the missionary methods of the friars.

The Spanish colonial system in the Philippines grew out of their experience in the Americas, and this in turn was developed out of their experience of *reconquista* of Spain from the Moors (Phelan 1959:4). As Phelan explains:

> The Spanish program in the Philippines envisaged a radical transformation of native Philippine society. Inspired by their previous experience in Mexico, the Spaniards launched a sweeping social reform in the islands, a reform which was religious, political, and economic in scope (1959:viii).

Two basic features of this system were the *encomienda* and the *reducción*. Let us look briefly at what these two terms meant in the Spanish Philippines.

The Encomienda

The *encomiendas,* or *repartimientos* as they were sometimes called, were feudal holdings granted by the King of Spain to the colonizers, often as rewards for faithful service to the Crown. These included land, natural resources and the right to labor and tribute from the inhabitants. The *encomendero* or holder of the estate was free, under certain restrictions, to exploit his *encomienda* for profit. He was put under obligation to fulfill certain responsibilities to the native population. Bishop Salazar (1591) pointed up these obligations as he quoted from the royal ordinances, section 144, drawn up in Segovia, Spain:

> When the country has been pacified, and its ruler and inhabitants have been reduced to obedience to us, the Governor shall, with their consent, direct the partition of the lands among the colonists so that each of them shall be responsible for the Indians of his repartimiento, defend and protect them and *provide a minister who shall teach them* to live in civilized ways, and shall do for them all else that encomenderos are bound to do for their Indians of their repartimientos (Blair, Robertson 1903:Vol. VIII, 285-286).

These *encomiendas* were more like dukedoms than strict land grants since the legal ownership of the land did not pass to the *encomendero*. The most important right was that of collecting tribute. Pre-Spanish Filipinos had been used to paying tribute to the *datus*, so the system itself did not seem utterly foreign to them. Besides the private *encomiendas* there were royal *encomiendas*, the purpose of which was to raise revenue for the government.

By 1591 there were 267 *encomiendas* scattered over the islands. The peak was reached in 1621 when it is reported that there were over 100,000, some of which were granted to prominent Filipinos as well as Spaniards. These tended to revert to the Crown, and the system slowly passed out of existence. During the early days, however, they were an important part of the Spanish colonial system.

Some *encomiendas* were very profitable. One *encomendero* is reported to have left an estate of more than 150,000 pesos from gains on cotton fabrics alone (Blair, Robertson 1903:Vol. XII, 188). More often, though, they proved unprofitable and caused real economic hardships in the country until the China trade got under way to take the pressure off. In trying to wring profits from these *encomiendas*, many owners began to use oppressive measures against the people. The system was ready-made for this type of abuse. But these abuses did not go unnoticed. Las Casas had done his work well. A disciple of his, Domingo Salazar, also a Dominican, became the first Bishop of Manila and the defender of the oppressed Filipino. He railed against the heartlessness of the *encomenderos* in a series of twenty-five *Conclusions* regarding the collection of tributes (Blair, Robertson 1903:Vol. VII, 276-288). He condemned the forcing of conversion "by the perversion of all law, divine and human, by murders, robberies, captivities, conflagrations, and the depopulations of villages, estates and houses." He concluded:

> Since the Spaniards entered the Indias, their excessive cupidities have devised new methods of preaching the gospel such as our Lord Jesus Christ never ordained or His holy Apostles knew; they are not permitted by the law of nature, nor do they agree with reason (Blair, Robertson 1903:Vol. VII, 288).

The *Conclusions* of Bishop Salazar clearly indicate that he felt that the primary task of the *encomenderos* was to see that the natives were Christianized. "It therefore follows," says Salazar, "that the *encomiendas* are and should be instituted rather for the good of the Indians than for that of the *encomenderos*" (Blair, Robertson 1930: Vol. VII, 282).

This idealistic view naturally raised the ire of the *encomenderos*. In a rather plaintive petition to the Governor they complained of living in "straitened circumstances" due to the unprofitableness of their *encomiendas*, and that

> in this state of affairs it seems that on the part of the bishop of these islands and some of the religious thereof – not only generally, in sermons and in the pulpit, but privately, in the confessional – obstacles and difficulties are imposed upon our consciences by maintaining that we cannot exact the [*illegible in MS*] his Majesty those which he exacts, and that we are going straight to hell. [*illegible in MS*] and that we are under obligation to make restitution for them (Blair, Robertson 1903:Vol. VII, 302).

In this tense situation the Governor was probably justified in asking Bishop Salazar to consider the *encomienda* the lesser of two evils – the other being the forfeiture of Spain's possession of the islands. The Governor was a realist and was pointing up the basic importance of the *encomienda* system in the process of Christianization of the Philippines. It was only through these holdings that the great early expansion of Roman Catholic Christianity took place. Through the *encomiendas* the early friars were immediately able to work among pacified and gainfully employed native groups. Instead of having to move slowly, *barangay* by *barangay,* they were able to evangelize a whole district. Finances and church buildings which otherwise would not have been provided were also provided through this system. The *encomienda* soon outlived its usefulness, but in the early days it was an important factor in the expansion of Christianity in the islands. The real lack, as Bishop Salazar himself pointed out, was that of friars to carry out the needed mission work. The openings were there, crying for men. In 1604 Friar Chirino, a Jesuit missionary, quoted another experienced missionary greeting some new arrivals as saying: "Would they were a thousand fathers, for they would all have a harvest in the Filipinas" (Blair, Robertson 1903:Vol. XII, 234).

The Reducción

The Spaniards were not men of small dreams. As Phelan says:

> The Spanish program in the Philippines envisaged a radical transformation of native Philippine society. Inspired by their previous experience in Mexico, the Spanish launched a sweeping social reform in the islands, a reform which was religious, political and economic in scope (1959:vii).

The fragmentary nature of Philippine baranganic society, with its multitude of small, independent settlements on the many islands of the archipelago, posed tremendous difficulties to the Spanish mission. Their solution, well tried out in the Americas, was to "reduce" the population. That is, the Filipinos would be resettled and gathered into compact villages and towns. Only in this way could government be effective and the Church firmly established. This process, known as *reducción,* must have seemed necessary in view of the "parish" nature of Roman Catholic Christianity. *"Reducción"* struck a vital nerve in early Philippine society, and the people reacted strongly. Their ancestral homes and lands were in the scattered *barangays,* and they tenaciously resisted resettlement.

An interesting case history of how a town was formed is found in a book produced by the Historical Conservation Society of the Philippines entitled *Majayjay (How a Town Came Into Being)* (Palazon 1964). The title of the first chapter is "The Malay Barangay Becomes a Town," but more accurately should be "Several Malay Barangays Become a Town." The story begins as Salcedo made his swing through Laguna. Apparently, the people of the area around present-day Majayjay gathered to oppose Salcedo. He, helped by some local allies, outflanked and defeated the local force. Majayjay was then given as an *encomienda* in 1578 to Gaspar Osorio de Morga, a soldier who had accompanied Legaspi and later became one of the early mayors of Manila. Some time later the decree of formation for the town was issued. The first *capitan* or *gobernadocillo* (little governor) on record was Don Agustin Osorio, who held office in 1597. It is conjectured that this was one of the *datus* of a former *barangay* who upon baptism took on the family name of the *encomendero*. If this is true, it illustrates the Spanish procedure of working through the local political leadership as much as possible.

In June, 1577, fourteen Franciscan friars arrived in Manila, two of whom immediately departed for China. One of those remaining was assigned to this area of Laguna. As a result of the labors of Friar Plasencia, Majayjay had become a true town by 1591. Although a church was built and the town organized, opposition to resettlement did not cease. According to a decree issued in 1621, some of the inhabitants would have both a town house and another house in the fields of another town. If asked to pay tribute in one town the citizen would reply that he had already paid tribute in the other, and vice versa. Finally the *audiencia,* the colonial supreme court, ordered the provincial governor to tear down the houses in the field (Palazon 1964). One can readily understand why this policy of *reducción* was the major source of social unrest in the seventeenth century.

The conflict seems to have resolved itself in a compromise. The Spaniards got their town, but the people tended to live in smaller groupings such as *sitios* (hamlets), *barrios* (villages) and districts of a town, reflecting the earlier baranganic structure. Wisely enough, the Spaniards continued to work through the native leadership. Former *datus* became the *cabezas de barangay* (heads of the *barangay*), whose task it was to collect the tribute.

In ordering church life the friars made some adjustments to the local pattern of dispersed living. They built larger town churches in what were then called *cabeceras,* or capitals of the parish. These were the home of the clergy and the focus of all the great religious festivals. In addition to these town churches were the *visita* chapels built in the smaller settlements, which received occasional visits from the priests. Anyone familiar with present-day Philippines has seen the town church-barrio chapel complex as the outgrowth of the original *cabecera-visita* pattern.

The Friars

The heart of the process of Christianization in the Philippines was not, however, the *encomienda* or the *reducción*. It was rather the missionaries themselves, the friars. It is here, too, that we see one of the strange twists of Philippine history. By universal testimony, the heroes of those early days were these dedicated monks who planted the Roman Catholic Church firmly throughout the islands. By 1898, however, the friars were the very symbol of all that was wrong and oppressive in the Spanish colonial regime. What went wrong is a subject for a later chapter. We want now to look at these early missionaries and what they accomplished.

Throughout much of the history of the Christian Church, the burden of the expansion of Christianity has fallen upon the monks. They are sometimes referred to as the "regular" clergy because they are bound together by a *regula* or rule, as distinguished from the "secular" clergy, who serve under bishops in the regular parish ministry. These disciplined, dedicated and often learned men were uniquely fitted for pioneering work. The period with which we are dealing falls immediately after the Reformation and the Council of Trent. The enthusiasm of the counter-Reformation still burned hot, especially among the Jesuits who came to the islands.

We have seen how the work began slowly with only a handful of Augustinians. Following pacification, however, Legaspi's successor, Governor Guilo de Lavezaris, urgently requested that more missionaries be sent of the different orders — especially Jesuits. The first to respond was a group of Franciscans who arrived in 1577 (see page 52). They opened missions around Laguna de Bay and then south into Camarines in Southern Luzon.

These were followed by the Jesuits, under Friar Sedeno as superior, who had just come to Mexico from a short and unsuccessful mission into Florida. The story of their arrival in the Philippines in 1581 gives us a glimpse into the hardiness of these early missionaries. They sailed from Mexico on the same ship as the first bishop to be appointed to the Philippines — Bishop Salazar, whom we have met before. When they arrived at what is now Sorsogon, at the southern tip of Luzon, they found the winds unfavorable for proceeding to Manila by ship. Bishop Salazar decided to go by land, although it was the rainy season and there were no roads. The sturdy priests walked up the Camarines peninsula, stopping at Franciscan missions along the way, where they no doubt enjoyed some good Spanish hospitality. Two months later, on September 17, 1581, they arrived in Manila. It was not much of a city then; only a cluster of about two hundred wooden houses.

The Dominicans followed in 1587, no doubt encouraged by Bishop Salazar, himself a Dominican. Later, in 1606, the Augustinian Recollects joined their forces to the growing number of missionaries of the various orders.

Although there were several noteworthy missionary friars during this period, Juan de Plasencia was the most outstanding of the early Franciscans. He composed a Tagalog Catechism which was examined and approved by the Synod of Manila and probably was the basis of the historic *Doctrina Cristiana,* printed in Roman and Tagalog characters in 1593. We have already referred to his famous description of pre-Spanish Tagalog society. This latter work was considered by the Spanish law courts to be the definitive statement of customary law. He was active in organizing towns in his area (by *reducción*) and promoted the spread of elementary education. He served among the Tagalogs in the Laguna de Bay area until his death in 1590 in Lilio, Laguna.

One of the most fascinating of these early monks was Friar Pedro Chirino. In the beginning, the Jesuit mission in the Philippines was an itinerant mission. That is, the friars would go on mission tours from town to town, as had been their custom in Europe. This proved impractical in the Philippine situation, so when Friar Chirino arrived in 1590 he brought with him permission to engage in resident missionary work. He became the first Jesuit to take up this kind of mission. In his book, the *Relation* (complete translation in Blair, Robertson 1903), he tells of his many and varied experiences as a missionary in various parts of the islands. This book is filled with the excitement of a pioneering work in a very responsive field. As we read of his accomplishments and sense his enthusiasm we can forgive his possible promotional bias.

Chirino began with a study of the Tagalog language. Like many another missionary, he became an enthusiast concerning his adopted language:

> I found in this language four qualities of the four greatest languages of the world, Hebrew, Greek, Latin and Spanish: It has the abstruseness and the obscurities of the Hebrew; the articles and distinctions in proper as well as in common nouns, of the Greek; the fulness and elegance of the Latin; and the refinement, polish, and the courtesy of the Spanish (Blair, Robertson 1903:Vol. XII, 236).

One may be sure that he has endeared himself to many generations of Tagalog speakers by these words of praise!

After a few months of language study, Chirino was called to Balayan, Batangas, to relieve the parish priest temporarily. It was a difficult time — a smallpox epidemic was raging — but he seems to have been well received and ministered much to the suffering families.

Then, after only two months, he was recalled and was asked to open the first Jesuit mission station in Taytay, about fifteen miles from Manila. This was to be part of a mission in a large *encomienda,* comprising not only Taytay, but also Antipolo and other small *barangays.* At the end of ten years, Chirino, in conscious imitation of St. Gregory the Miracle-worker, stated that "when I entered the place, I found hardly forty Christians, and at the end of that time there were not four infidels" (Blair, Robertson 1903: Vol. XII, 205).

He tells of miraculous happenings, healings and outstanding conversions. One of the most colorful of the conversions was that of a "wild man," Sayor ("Robber") by name. He lived in the caves of the mountains and was a mighty hunter. Deer, wild boar and, on occasion, the giant python were his prey. When he would enter a village everyone would flee, and he would help himself to whatever he desired. One day this man, clothed only in a G-string and armed with a dagger, holding a bow and arrows in his hand, approached Friar Chirino. Chirino relates, "I caressed him, and tried to soften him with presents and gentle treatment" (Blair, Robertson 1903: Vol. XII, 258). Sayor began to visit the friar regularly. He regaled him with stories of his hunting exploits, while the priest in turn instructed him in Christian doctrine. Soon Sayor was so taken with his new friend (probably the first man to treat him as a human being) that he appointed himself Chirino's bodyguard on mission trips. Several years after Chirino was transferred from the area, Sayor moved into town, was baptized, married and became a pillar of the church. He took great pride in his Christian name "Pablo," so that if addressed "Sayor," he would answer "not Sayor, but Pablo!"

Chirino moved on from Taytay to the Visayan Islands, studied a new language and conducted a successful mission there.

Missionary Methods

Protestant writers have too often written off Spanish missionary methods as a simple combination of the Cross and the Sword — with the emphasis upon the latter. What we have seen of the work of the early friars would indicate that this type of generalization is grossly unfair. Let us then look a little more carefully at the way the Spanish went about the Christianization of the Filipinos.

Their missionary methods may be summarized in seven general points:

1. The missionaries themselves were the primary agents of the spread of Roman Catholic Christianity. This means there was a clear division between the civil agents of the State and the religious. There was even a distinction within the clergy itself. It was the regular priests, the friars, who were responsible for the extension of the Faith. This had some important advantages in the Philippine situation, for the friars were missionary specialists under discipline. Their purpose was to establish the Church among the native population. They did not become chaplains only for the Spanish population. This contrasts favorably with the very early Protestant missionary efforts conducted by chaplains of the trading companies. In the long run, however, this method tends to produce a highly dependent type of national Church.

2. The missionary friars worked through the Spanish colonial system. They were intimately involved in the whole *encomienda-reducción* program of colonization. This must have seemed quite natural, as the union of Church and State was to them axiomatic. It also proved helpful to their efforts. Force could be used against recalcitrant natives. Chirino, for example, relates the story of a lady who was restrained from receiving baptism by her husband. She reported him, and he was forthwith arrested. The woman was baptized and "within a few days he [the husband] returned to the church, subdued and was baptized" (Blair, Robertson 1903:Vol. XIII, 161f.). This type of use of force seemed acceptable to them, but actual forced conversion was against the stated policy, though some were reported.

The mission of the friars no doubt was made much easier by the Spanish military superiority in the islands. The ships in the harbors and the armament of the soldiers surely created an atmosphere of Spanish power and a feeling among the Filipinos of the hopelessness of resistance. In the physical "power encounter" the Spanish were clearly the victors. In the cultural encounter, also, primitive Philippine culture could not compete with the more advanced Western civilization of the Spaniards.

3. The available personnel were widely dispersed through the islands. An extensive rather than intensive principle of missionary deployment was adopted. This enabled a few missionaries to work widely among a relatively large population.

4. The friars worked with the people in their own languages. This was true, as we have seen, from the beginning. The Synod of Manila (1581-1586) in its one decision on missionary methods made it the official policy that "the native catechumens were to be instructed in their own language rather than Spanish" (de la Costa 1961:31). In this way and in others, the early friars showed their basic respect for the indigenous cultures. The use of the native languages leads naturally to the next point.

5. There was a strong emphasis upon instruction. When Friar Chirino moved into Taytay, he immediately organized catechism classes for children which met every morning after mass. He first taught the children the basic prayers, then the catechism. The adults were then incorporated into these classes, and sometimes a youngster would even be assigned to instruct an elderly person. Post-baptismal classes also were conducted.

Both the importance of instruction and the dangers of its neglect were emphasized by Bishop Salazar in 1591:

> When the minister undertakes to baptize them, he must see that they know well what it is, and are prepared for it and understand what they are receiving — namely, that they are dead to their past life, and are commencing a new one, and from that time forth are new men. As the inhabitants of many of these islands have received baptism without the aforesaid solicitude and preparation, many sacrileges have been committed; and as a result, many and great misfortunes have ensued, which we can now clearly discern, and yet but poorly remedy (Blair, Robertson 1903:Vol. VII, 279).

Then as now, mission policy and mission practice must not have always coincided. In this task of instructing a large body of scattered converts, some friars wisely used certain native catechists who worked among the *visitas*.

Both Morga and Chirino mention that baptism was actually postponed in certain districts for lack of instruction, which in turn was due to a lack of priests.

6. In their preaching, the friars used what might be termed a very direct approach. They did not hesitate to identify the *anitos* (spirits) of the ancient religion with demons. They demanded the complete destruction of all of the old images and religious paraphernalia. Chirino relates that "one of ours [i.e., a Jesuit] converted many of them by means of a well painted picture of hell" (Blair, Robertson 1903:Vol. XIII, 264). One used hot coals as "visual aids." Syncretism was resisted and there were definite power encounters between Christianity and paganism.

A striking case occurred in Taytay. A priestess (a *katalonan*) went about secretly telling the people that her *anito* was a very close friend of the *anito* of the Christians. She had much influence until the priest found out about it. He searched her home for the image, but found none at first. The *anito* supposedly had told the woman that he would never be found. However, the priest suddenly suspected a cane prop supporting the ridge pole of the roof. He ordered it cut down, and in it he found the small gold image he had been looking for. Chirino relates that "the demon was so insulted" that he began to torment the woman. Already disillusioned, the priestess begged for mercy and was given a cross as a defense. The terror continued for a short time, then suddenly ceased. The woman confessed publicly, and a general destruction of idols followed.

7. Wherever possible, indigenous forms were used. Working with, not against, native culture was a basic feature of much of Roman Catholic, and especially Jesuit, missionary work of this period. Chirino made use of ancient Tagalog chant tunes to teach the catechism to the children. One wonders if this may not be the origin of the present-day singing of the *Pasyon* (Story of the Life and Death of Christ) during Holy Week. Native social etiquette was observed — as when Chirino and the *datus* of Valayan tried to outdo each other in ceremonial bowing! In these and other ways, the missionaries tried to minimize the cultural changes involved in becoming a Christian.

These methods need to be evaluated critically, but before we can do that, we must look first at what the missionaries, using these methods, actually accomplished.

ROMAN CATHOLIC CHURCH GROWTH

The study of church growth, that is, the growth of a particular Church (denomination) in a particular society, is rapidly becoming a scholarly discipline in its own right. Its tool of study is the graph of growth, and it draws on the disciplines of history, sociology and anthropology in its interpretation of this graph. Some may doubt the validity of applying these techniques to the type of situation with which we are dealing here, since the outcome seems to be predetermined. However, the Roman Catholic Church did grow in the Philippines and this growth is subject to investigation. Having said this, one must add that this growth was a very special kind of growth in a very special kind of situation.

Actual Growth

The basic facts are quickly told. The following table and accompanying graph show the slow beginning, followed by a period of great growth, until by 1630 the majority of the lowland, pacified population was baptized. Population figures of the graph are from Blair, Robertson 1903:Vol. I, 86. The sources of growth figures are Phelan (1959:56) and Latourette (1939:Vol. III, 312).

Table of Growth — Roman Catholic Church
1570 – 100   Baptized
1583 – 100,000
1586 – 146,700 (Phelan – 170,000)
1594 – 286,000
1612 – 322,400
1629 – 500,000
1735 – 837,182
1750 – 904,116

In terms of *types* of growth, the records would indicate that in the period before 1630, the major source of growth was what is termed *conversion* growth — that is, growth which resulted from conversion from paganism. This is somewhat clouded by the emphasis of the early missionaries on baptizing children, apparently whether or not the parents had yet been baptized. They were able to operate in this way only because of their security as the colonizing power. After 1630, and probably somewhat before that date, *biological* growth (that is, addition through the growth of the Christian families) was the primary factor.

There were still pockets of paganism which were won over during this time, however, so there was some conversion growth taking place. It is to be understood that the word "conversion" here is used as a Roman Catholic would understand it.

The Reasons for Growth

What were the reasons for this very rapid growth? A modern Catholic writer, Regan (1957:12), gives three reasons for what he terms this "phenomenal success":

1. The King of Spain, Philip II, desired ardently the conversion of the Filipinos.
2. The missionaries were zealous.
3. The Filipinos were a naturally religious people.

Anthropologist Frank Lynch, S. J. (1955:477) gives a similar set of reasons stated more carefully and less promotionally:

1. Official Spanish policy under King Philip II placed spiritual objectives before commercial.
2. Earliest missionaries were men of extraordinary zeal.
3. No highly structured religious system to oppose the innovations proposed by the missionaries.
4. Little resistance to small show of arms, little bloodshed.

We can gain some insight through the above lists, but it would seem that many things are yet unexplained. Why, for example, were the mountain tribes, with somewhat similar religious structures, so highly resistant? It would seem most helpful to analyze the reasons for growth in terms of the historical, sociological and religious factors involved.

1. Historical reasons:

a. Spain's armed conquest of the Philippines, combined with a lack of interference by other foreign powers. The Dutch interference did not begin until about 1610.

b. This was Spain's only colony in the Far East, so she was able to concentrate her forces on this one area.

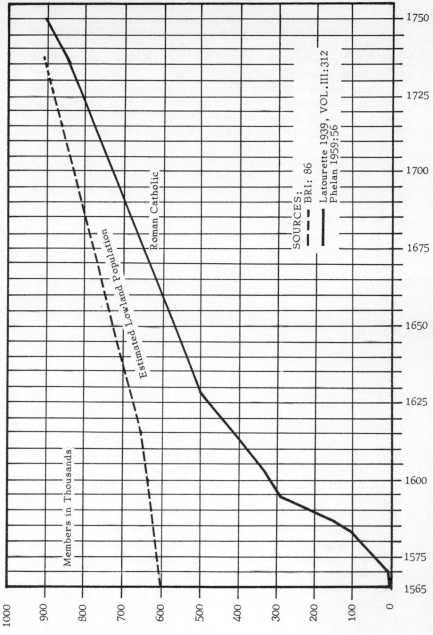

FIGURE 2   Growth Roman Catholic Church 1565-1750

c. The lack of great economic incentives to exploitation of the islands.

d. The fact of the prior bloody conquests in Latin America and King Philip II's determination that the conquest of the Philippines should be accomplished with a minimum of bloodshed.

e. The fact that the Moslem intrusion into the Philippines was only beginning at the time of the Conquest.

f. The apparent readiness for change of the majority of the lowland population at that time.

g. The absolutely irresistible force which Spanish ships armed with cannon brought to bear on coastal villages. Resistance was impossible, and acceptance of Spain meant acceptance of Spain's religion.

2. Sociological reasons:

a. The fragmentary nature of early baranganic society. The early Filipinos could not effectively unite to resist Spanish conquest.

b. The willingness of the Spanish missionaries to accept much of the early Philippine social structure. The authority of the *datus* was not directly undermined, though it gradually weakened as the towns developed.

c. The decision to work in the native languages.

d. The predominantly monogamous pattern of marriage. The easy divorce of early Philippine society posed a problem later, however.

e. The basic similarity of the different lowland peoples made the task much easier. The people movement mechanisms, which will be discussed below, stopped at the more isolated mountain tribal groups and the Moslem groups of the south.

f. The lowland peoples were already quite innovative due to frequent migrations and contacts with the outside world.

3. Religious reasons:

a. The undoubted dedication and ability of the early missionaries.

b. The animistic religion of the early Filipinos was not highly structured. There were no great temples or concentration of wealth in the religious leaders. There was no highly organized hierarchy to oppose the spread of Christianity.

c. The appeal of the colorful ceremonies of the Roman Catholic Faith.

d. The superiority of the Roman Catholic teachings over the

animistic beliefs was apparent. Morga reports that the people showed "good understanding" in accepting the truths of the Christian religion, and regarded the teachings as good (Blair, Robertson 1903:Vol. XVI, 150).

e. Miracles, supposed or real, validated the Spanish claim of the superior power of the Christian God over the spirits (demons) of the native religion.

f. The zeal of the early missionaries in seeing that all the images and relics of the ancient religion were destroyed.

In point e under the sociological reasons above we mentioned "people movement mechanisms." We now want to ask if this rapid growth of Roman Catholic Christianity can properly be termed a people movement. According to Dr. Donald M. McGavran (1955) a people movement can be defined as follows:

> It is a movement involving multi-individual, mutually inter-dependent decisions to accept Christianity within a homo-geneous segment of society (a tribe or caste, a people).

Does what happened in the Philippines meet the criteria for a people movement? A large number of people over a short period of time did accept Christianity as it was presented to them. These people were able to become Christians without moving out of their social group, especially as the movement grew. Chirino quotes Friar Juan de San Lucas as saying:

> It seems to me that the road to the conversion of those natives is now smooth and open, with the conversion of the chiefs and of the majority of the people; for the excuse which they formerly gave, saying, "I will become a Christian as soon as the rest do," has now become their incentive toward conversion, and they now say: "We desire to become Christians because all the rest are Christians" (Blair, Robertson 1903:Vol. XIII, 161).

The question now remaining is whether this was growth in a single homogeneous unit. As there were different language and tribal groups on different islands and in different areas, it must be said that there was not just one homogeneous unit, although the lowland cultures were quite similar, as we have emphasized. It would then be more accurate to say that what we are dealing with is a series of people movements in very similar societies. The fact of this growth taking place under the pressure of an aggressive, colonizing power clouds the picture considerably. The family structure would seem to favor more of a web-type people movement than what we see actually occurring. We may conclude that we are indeed dealing with hundreds of people movements of a special type.

Another dimension in this study can be added by noticing the dynamics of communication in a society such as we are dealing with here. Dr. Eugene Nida has emphasized the importance of social structure (by which he especially means class structure) in understanding communication within a society. He notes that "communication never takes place in a social vacuum, but always between individuals who are part of a total social context" (1960:94). A colonial society is basically a totalitarian society. How does communication take place in this type of society? Nida says, from the top down and then out to the edges of the society. Picturing early Philippine society as a diamond-shaped social structure, we can visualize the process of communication in this way:

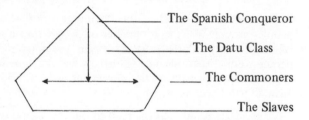

The Spanish Conqueror

The Datu Class

The Commoners

The Slaves

We are dealing, then, with the special type of people movement which occurs in totalitarian societies. This picture is somewhat modified by the few cases of actual forced conversions. But the fact remains that missions in the modern post-colonial age cannot expect this kind of growth. Communism, however, is experiencing this type of growth in some parts of the world.

THE MIDDLE COLONIAL PERIOD (1610–1812)

For the purposes of our study we need not tarry long in this period. The period of great growth was now in the past. Conversion growth did occur on a small scale as the missionaries pressed the work of Christianization out to the edges of the pacified groups. By 1700, this work was effectively completed. Efforts were made to enter the Moslem areas, but soon were abandoned. Work was also

begun among some of the mountain tribal groups, but little progress
was made.

In church growth terminology, conversion growth should have
been followed by "perfection" growth during this period. Any
large-scale movement into Christianity tends to sweep large numbers
of untaught, superficially committed people into the Christian
community. This does not mean that such movements are bad in
themselves, but it does mean that a people movement needs to be
consummated by a period of solid Christian instruction and deep
spiritual awakening. In the Philippines, however, the weaknesses of
the Spanish program became more apparent as time went on. The
inner dynamic of a vital Christian faith based upon the Bible was
largely lacking. In its place was a ritualistic, authoritarian and
externalized form of Christianity that was often too hospitable to
former pagan beliefs and superstitions.

The "Golden Age" then quickly came to an end. Its close was
marked by the beginning of the Dutch attacks in 1609. These
attacks continued until 1648 when Spain formally recognized Dutch
independence. The British invaded the islands and actually held
them from 1762 until 1764. The demoralizing effects of these
attacks from without were compounded by the savage Moro attacks
from the Moslem areas of the south.

Internally, the mission work suffered from a chronic shortage of
priests, lack of discipline and rivalry between factions within the
Church. The Augustinians faced a grave disciplinary crisis that
reached its climax in 1617 when the provincial superior, Sepulveda,
was murdered by a group of disgruntled monks. The Jesuits had to
discipline several members for immoral conduct. The high optimism
of the early period gave way to discouragement in the second
generation of missionaries. The old pagan beliefs showed great
tenacity.

The so-called "Visitation Controversy" continued to demand the
attention of the various prelates throughout the entire period. The
issue was whether the Bishop had the authority to "visit" or oversee
the "regular" clergy who occupied so many of the parishes of the
country.

There was friction between the various orders themselves, in spite
of the royal edict of 1594 in which King Philip II directed that

because I have learned that better results will be obtained by assigning each order to a district by itself ... I command you ... that where Augustinians go there shall be no Franciscans, nor religious of the Society where there are Dominicans. Thus you will proceed assigning each order to its province (Blair, Robertson 1903:Vol. IX, 120f.).

As time went on the Orders obtained more and more property and power. By not encouraging the development of a native clergy they extended the period of "mission" too long and eventually set the stage for the great revolt against the friars at the end of the nineteenth century. This tendency to extend the period of mission too long has been characteristic of Roman Catholic missions in non-European countries. Even today, for example, Latin America is heavily dependent upon foreign priests, even though the Roman Catholic Church in that part of the world is over four hundred years old. Protestant missions should take warning from the Roman Catholic experience in this matter.

The picture was not all dark, however. The Christianized majority remained faithful to the Church. The ideal of the Christian family was accepted. Educational and medical institutions were established, especially in Manila.

So, in spite of attacks from without and difficulties within, the basic accomplishments of the first missionaries remained. They had established a Roman Catholic nation in Asia — to this day, the only Christian nation in the Orient.

AN EVANGELICAL EVALUATION

Soon after the American acquisition of the Philippines, the Yale historian, Edward Gaylord Bourne, wrote:

It is customary, too, for Protestant writers to speak with contempt of Catholic missions, but it must not be forgotten that France and England were converted to Christianity by similar methods. The Protestant ridicules the wholesale baptisms and conversions and a Christianity not even skindeep, but that was the way in which Christianity was once propagated in what are the ruling Christian nations of today. The Catholic, on the other hand, might ask for some evidence that the early Germans, or the Anglo-Saxons would ever have been converted to Christianity by the methods employed by Protestants. . . .

In the light, then, of impartial history raised above race prejudice and religious prepossessions, after a comparison with the early years of the Spanish conquest in America or with the first generation or two of the English settlements, the conversion and civilization of the Philippines in the forty years following Legaspi's arrival must be pronounced an achievement without parallel in history (Blair, Robertson 1903:Vol. I, 37).

Bourne's strictures against the common Protestant criticism of Roman Catholic missions are no doubt in the main deserved. One doubts, however, whether the strictly "impartial history" of which he speaks exists. Each historian sees history from his own peculiar standpoint. As a conservative evangelical Christian, this author must evaluate what he himself has recorded in the light of his own personal beliefs and experiences. What can an evangelical say concerning the story of the Spanish Conquest and Christianization of the Philippines?

First of all, we must recognize the providential timing of the Spanish arrival. If the islands had gone to Islam, the whole history of missions in this area would have been different, and evangelization immensely more difficult.

We salute the dedication of the early Spanish missionaries. Their appreciation of the native culture can only be praised. Their lack of feelings of racial superiority is notable. The stories of the power encounters between Christianity and paganism in the experiences of the early friars must be seriously considered by the modern evangelical as actual power encounters between God and Satan, as the early friars considered them to be.

It is at this point, however, that deep questions arise in the evangelical's mind. When the early Filipinos gave up their idols, what was given in their place? A superior faith, it is not to be doubted. But was it the pure gospel of grace as it is revealed in Scripture? Personal living faith in a present Savior was not stressed. A notable failure of the Roman Catholic mission was that during the entire 333 years of Spanish control not a single translation of the Bible was made into any of the languages of the islands. Catechisms there were, Bibles there were not. When they destroyed their images, did the people simply consider the cross a more powerful image? The use of the cross to protect a field of grain from locusts indicates that they may have.

This is not to charge the early priests with promoting syncretism. The records indicate that they were very aware of this danger, at least in its grosser forms. However, the lack of priests and the failure to develop a strong national clergy resulted in an undershepherded people in which many of the ancient vices and superstitions were very much alive.

It has been said that a people movement is a fine place to begin but a poor place to end. This could well be a commentary on the Spanish period of the history of the Philippines. Roman Catholic doctrine and church structure made it impossible to give proper pastoral care to the people. The lack of Scriptures and of religious freedom made it impossible for any spiritual renewal to take place. This had to await the day when the Spanish grip on the Philippines finally was broken.

PART II

THE INTRODUCTION OF PROTESTANT CHRISTIANITY INTO THE PHILIPPINES

CHAPTER 5

THE PHILIPPINE REVOLUTION
AND THE AMERICAN ACQUISITION
OF THE PHILIPPINES

The first great turning point in Philippine religious life was the entrance of Roman Catholic Christianity over four hundred years ago, which we have considered in some detail in Chapter 4. We consider now the second major religious crisis, that of the entrance of Protestant Christianity at the turn of the twentieth century. Again we want to see this event in its full historical and sociological environment. American missionaries, especially, should understand the Hispanic-Malayan nature of the society of this period as well as the role of the United States in the revolution. Present-day Philippine nationalism cannot be understood without this background. The religious aspect of the history of this period is so important that the political history and the religious history of the Philippines practically merge. The prominent activity of the friars through these years illustrates this. The history, then, that we will discuss, and the sociology that we will study, are not "mere" history or sociology. Rather they are the necessary guides to understanding what was happening in the early days of Protestant Christianity in the Philippines.

As we move now into the latter part of the nineteenth century to begin the story of the entrance of Protestant Christianity into the Philippines, we see a radically different world than that of the latter part of the sixteenth century when Roman Catholic Christianity entered. The age of exploration had passed. The Industrial Revolution had occurred. A new nation, the United States of America, had come onto the scene and was becoming a world power. Protestant missions were in their Great Century. And Spain was struggling to preserve the last remnants of her once great, globe-encircling empire. Through a policy of trade restriction and religious intolerance, Spain had sought to insulate the Philippines from the many forces of change which were moving so powerfully through the world. But a new age had arrived and history was not to be stopped. Radical change was to come to the Philippines — though only through internal revolution and foreign armed intervention.

At least three conditions must exist before a revolution can occur. First, there must be some sense of national identity. The people must feel that they are a unity and can move together if necessary. Second, there must be a basic dissatisfaction with the status quo that is widespread enough to give the revolution a base of support, and deep enough to provide the motivation to carry it through. Third, there must be a small group of leaders, an elite, who can focus and direct the mass force in a revolutionary movement.

Throughout the early history of Spanish rule there had been numerous sporadic uprisings against Spanish domination. Most of these were local outbursts against particular instances of Spanish oppression. They were symptoms of social unrest, but they did not envisage the actual overthrow of the Spanish regime. Thus they were not actually revolutionary in nature.

In the nineteenth century, however, a true Philippine nationalism arose. Fanned by the ideas of liberty and justice, and stiffened by the oppressive forces of a frightened Spanish minority, this movement culminated in the revolution of 1896. The tragedy of this drama lies in the fact that the part of the villain was played by the friars. The irony lies partly in the fact that it was this very group which had been the primary instrument of the spread throughout the islands of the Hispanic culture and the Roman Catholic Faith, which provided the common cultural base for the rise of this pan-Philippine nationalism.

It has been said that power corrupts, and absolute power corrupts absolutely. Through the centuries of Spanish rule the friars had become more and more powerful, until in the nineteenth century they were actually the ruling power. In the person of the friar, Church and State were visibly united, especially for the average citizen of a provincial town. As the *encomiendas* were dissolved, the orders acquired more and more lands, especially in Luzon. At the time of the revolution the extent of the friar lands reached to a total of 403,713 acres (Foreman 1906:601).

After the Napoleonic Wars, certain government reforms were instituted in Spain, beginning in 1810. A Philippine deputy was admitted to the Spanish Cortes (national legislative body). Foreman believes that it was by their adamant opposition to these and any reforms which threatened their privileged position that the friars themselves caused the rise of the infamous "friar question" (1906:362). (This term refers to the whole complex of complaints which finally ignited the Philippine revolution against Spain.) But the Philippines simply could not be completely insulated from the outside world. Liberal ideas began to seep into the country. When Mexico achieved independence in 1819, her close tie with the Philippines, which had been forged by two centuries of galleon trade, was finally broken. The Philippines was then brought into the European, and especially Spanish, trade market. By 1834 there was unrestricted foreign trade through Manila. Various European and American trading firms established themselves in the islands.

The forces for change were beginning to gain momentum. In the years from 1859 to 1872 several important events occurred. The Jesuits, who had been expelled in 1768, returned in 1859. Under strict instructions to limit their work to education and missionary work among the uncivilized tribes, they moved into Mindanao. This laudable move set in motion an unfortunate set of reactions. The Augustinian Recollects, who were previously in charge of the mission in Mindanao, were given parishes in Cavite, near Manila. Moving into these parishes, they replaced Filipino secular priests. This move created intense resentment, for not only was it against church law as defined by the Council of Trent, but it was "flagrant racial favoritism" (Laubach 1925:95).

The year 1869 marked the opening of the famed Suez Canal. Manila was brought within 32 days of Spain. Not only was trade with the mother country made easier, but the flow of students to Spain was greatly increased, particularly after the inauguration of regular steamship service in 1873.

The third great event of these years was the overthrow in 1868 of Queen Isabella and the establishment of the Spanish Republic for two significant years. A new governor-general, General de la Torre, was sent to Manila. He instituted many reforms which were gratefully welcomed by the Filipinos. Liberal ideas came in like a flood, and though the break in the dike was quickly closed with the restoration of the monarchy in 1870, the "damage" had been done. Filipinos, such as Dr. Burgos and the replaced priests of Cavite, began to agitate for reform. Repression could only lead to violence.

THE CAVITE MUTINY (1872)

Violence came quickly. The new governor, General Izquierdo, declared that he came to the Philippines "with a crucifix in one hand and a sword in the other" (Zaide 1958:171). One of the repressive measures he took was the withdrawal of longstanding privileges of workers at the arsenal at Cavite. These privileges included exemption from the payment of tribute and from forced labor. The Filipino soldiers made common cause with the workers and mutinied on the night of January 20, 1872.

It is reported that the uprising was to have been coordinated with a similar uprising in Manila. Unfortunately Sampaloc, Manila, was celebrating its fiesta the night of January 20, and the troops across the bay in Cavite mistook the fireworks for the signal. The mutiny was quickly and forcefully put down. Arrested for complicity in this mutiny were eleven Filipino priests, in addition to several lawyers and other prominent Filipinos. It has been charged that the friars engineered the whole uprising to implicate these men. However, it seems more likely that the friars saw their opportunity to rid themselves of some political enemies by implicating them in what they tried to make out to be a treasonable plot against the government. The case was tried by a military court and on February 17, 1872, three of the priests, the aggressive Dr. Burgos, the 84-year-old Padre Gomez, and Padre Zamora, who had been falsely accused, were executed by garrote (strangulation) on the Bagumbayan field, now called the Luneta, in Manila. A sort of poetic justice can be seen in the execution also of the false witness, Saldua, who may have been put up to this by the friars. Two others were put to death, ten were imprisoned, and nineteen were exiled to the Marianas (Alip 1947:Vol. II, 63).

Although there is little doubt that the friars had been active in pressing for the conviction of these men, the archbishop refused to defrock the three priests before their execution. But the fact that the friars could perpetrate such a deed points to a fatal defect in the religious system of which they were a part. The desperate overreaction of the government at this point only served to foster what they feared most: the eventual revolt of the colony against Spain. The coming revolutionary movement already had its martyrs. Only a few years later, Dr. Jose Rizal would also die a martyr's death on the same Bagumbayan field.

THE PROPAGANDA MOVEMENT (1872–1892)

The cruel suppression of the Cavite Mutiny was "neither forgotten nor forgiven" (Foreman 1906:363). The opposition to Spain entered a new phase. Political exiles met with students who had gone abroad. Among these Philippine expatriates a movement of protest was born, the so-called "Propaganda Movement."

Able men began to produce works of powerful protest against the cruelties of the Spanish oppression. A newspaper called *La Solidaridad* was begun in Barcelona, Spain, and became the official organ of this movement. This was a movement for reform, not revolution. Some of the greatest Filipinos of that generation were enlisted in this cause. The great lawyer and journalist, Marcelo H. del Pilar, became editor of the paper. Lopez Jaena was the orator of the movement. But by far the greatest of the leaders was Jose Rizal.

Jose Rizal, the Philippines' greatest son and hero, was born in Calamba, Laguna, on June 19, 1861. Under the tutelage of his gifted mother, Rizal showed precocious literary ability. He was reading in the Spanish Bible before he was five years old, and at eight wrote his first poem. He then saw his mother arrested under false charges, and about the same time learned of the execution of the three priests through his brother, Paciano, who had studied under the popular Dr. Burgos. Thus early in life he experienced the cruelty of the Spanish regime.

At the age of eleven he was sent off to Manila to study at the Ateneo de Manila, which was under the Jesuits. Later he attended the University of Santo Tomas, a Dominican school, as a medical student. It was here that he may have met Gregorio Aglipay who was later to become the founder of the Philippine Independent Church. Rizal came to appreciate the Jesuits and their system of education, which he contrasted so devestatingly with the medieval system of the Dominicans in his book *El Filibusterismo* (Rizal 1956b:126ff.).

In 1882 he realized that he was in some danger because of his radical views, so he escaped to Spain. There he became a Mason and was soon writing under the pen name "Laong Laan" (always prepared). Immersing himself in his studies, he carried on courses in medicine, philosophy and letters simultaneously. Inspired by Harriet Beecher Stowe's *Uncle Tom's Cabin,* and encouraged by his newly found friend, Blumentritt, an Austrian-Spanish ethnologist, Rizal decided to write a novel depicting the cruelties and racial arrogance of the Spanish in the Philippines. *Noli Me Tangere* (Touch Me Not) (1956a) was the result. As a novel this book has been both praised and criticized, but as a social protest tract it must be considered one of the most powerful. As might be expected, the villain of the plot is a rapacious friar; here again the religious roots of the discontent are emphasized.

In 1888 Rizal came home for six months, but his book had made it much too dangerous for him to stay, so he left again. This time he traveled through America, and then proceeded to England. There in the British Museum he hunted up a copy of Morga's *Sucesos* (see page 35). Appreciating the favorable light it cast on the early Filipinos, Rizal copied it and had it published with his notes at his own expense. His second novel *El Filibusterismo* followed. The oppression of his family and friends by the friars in Calamba is graphically told, using fictitious names. Pessimism is the note of this book, which was written after he realized bitterly that his childhood sweetheart was forever lost to him.

Rizal then moved to Hong Kong, where he set up practice as an oculist. One of the great joys of his life was to be able to operate on the cataracts in his mother's eyes. While in Hong Kong he wrote the constitution for the Liga Filipina (Philippine League), a civic organization that was to be formed in the Philippines for the purpose of promoting peaceful reform. After this he returned to Manila. The Liga was organized on July 3, 1892. Only four days later Rizal was arrested on suspicion of sedition and was exiled to Dapitan, a small southern island.

The exile of Rizal to Dapitan effectively ended the Propaganda movement, although *La Solidaridad* continued in Madrid for three more years. The importance of Rizal, however, lies not only in his political views. For although he never renounced Catholicism, his writings prepared the people of the Philippines for the coming of Protestantism. He was a fervent believer in freedom of thought, speech and investigation, especially in religious matters. He appealed to the people to think of the religion which they saw and were taught and compare it with the pure religion of Jesus. He told them to beware of the friars and to accept only what was acceptable to reason. Many Protestants may object to his rationalism, but his writings carried much force with his countrymen. People whose minds had been opened by Rizal were usually ready to listen to the Scriptures.

Politically, Rizal never advocated armed insurrection, yet his arrest in 1892 marked the beginning of the Revolutionary Movement. Majul explains why this was so:

> The Philippine Revolution was made possible by the very simple reason that many of the most intelligent, sensitive, and vocal Filipinos discovered that their demands on Colonial authorities for changes in the Colonial institutions in the country were not realizable (1960:5).

THE REVOLUTIONARY MOVEMENT (1892–1896)

Andres Bonifacio and the Katipunan

On the night of July 7, 1892, as Rizal was being arrested by Governor Despujol, another meeting was being held in Tondo, Manila. Andres Bonifacio and some friends were founding a secret revolutionary society, the Kataastaasang Kagalanggalang Katipunan Ng Mga Anak Ng Bayan (Highest and Most Respected Sons of the People), commonly known as the Katipunan or the K.K.K. The *ilustrados* (like Rizal) had formed the ideas, but it was a man of the masses, Bonifacio, who initiated the revolutionary movement (Majul 1960:10). The Katipunan was a secret society which patterned itself after Masonry. Members were initiated by the historic "blood pact." Clearly a revolutionary movement, it had a flag, a constitution and an embryonic government. It also proceeded to gather arms.

Desiring the backing of Rizal, the Katipunan leaders sent a delegation to see him in Dapitan. Believing the situation to be hopeless, Rizal refused to endorse the movement. Disappointed but not discouraged, Bonifacio continued to press forward with his society. The Katipunan made a futile request to Japan for arms. Meanwhile, rumors of the movement were circulating among the Spaniards. The Governor-general paid little attention at first, but the friars began to pressure him to move strongly against the movement. This instituted what Agoncillo terms a "war of nerves" (1956:136). Finally, on August 19, 1896, a young member of the Katipunan lost his nerve and confessed the secrets of the society to Friar Mariano

Gil, the hated Augustinian parish priest of Tondo. Whether or not this man's sister had previously confessed in the confessional could not be proved, though the Roman Catholic historian Zaide feels strongly that the friar did not break the secrecy of the confessional (Zaide 1939:91). In any event the secret was out, and many raids were carried out that night.

Following the discovery of the Katipunan by Friar Gil, Bonifacio gathered his forces in the hills of Balintawak, north of Manila. Here, on August 26, 1896, he took out his *cédula* (tax certificate) and tore it up. His followers followed suit, shouting "Long Live Philippine Independence!" — the famous "Cry of Balintawak."

The first battle was joined four days later at San Juan del Norte. Bonifacio, leading a large band of *katipuneros,* attacked a Spanish powder magazine. When Spanish reinforcements arrived from Manila, Bonifacio was forced to retreat. The next day, August 31, Aguinaldo, a young leader in Cavite, led an uprising in Kawit, Cavite, and here the revolutionaries were victorious. More victories followed in Cavite and this greatly enhanced Aguinaldo's prestige in the movement and paved the way for his eventual takeover.

The Martyrdom of Rizal

In the meantime, Rizal had volunteered to go to Cuba as a doctor for the Spanish Army. He was allowed to proceed to Spain, but before arrival he was placed under arrest, so that when he arrived in Barcelona, he was immediately sent back to the Philippines. He was tried by a military court, and although he insisted that he had nothing to do with the revolutionary movement, he was sentenced to die before a firing squad on December 30, 1896. Before his death he wrote his very patriotic and moving *Mi Ultimo Adios* (My Final Farewell). At six o'clock in the morning of December 30, 1898, the deed was done. Rizal, the "Pride of the Malay Race" (Palma), was now Rizal the Martyr.

By this act the Spanish sealed their fate in the Philippines. The point of no return had been reached, although the giggling Spanish ladies and the Loyalists shouting "*Viva la España!*" at the execution were unaware of this fact. The Spanish could never be forgiven, and independence would come — though not without foreign intervention.

THE REVOLUTION OF 1896 — AN APPARENT FAILURE

As a revolutionary movement expressing the anger of an oppressed people, the Revolution of 1896 could not be finally put down. But without adequate arms and military force, neither could it be victorious. It is important to note that the execution of Rizal did not "trigger" the revolution of 1896 (Wolff 1961:13), but rather stimulated the spirit to carry it through.

General Polavieja, who arrived just before the execution of Rizal, pressed the campaign against the insurgents vigorously. By the end of March, much of Cavite had been recaptured. In April, however, the ironfisted Polavieja was replaced by General de Rivera, who extended the olive branch of amnesty to those who would surrender. This new policy was to succeed — temporarily.

Meanwhile, the revolutionary movement itself was racked by a power struggle between the fiery Bonifacio and the more successful and dignified soldier, Emilio Aguinaldo. At the Taheros Assembly, a new revolutionary government replaced the Katipunan, and Aguinaldo was made President. Then followed a sordid episode in which Andres Bonifacio and his brother were courtmartialed by Aguinaldo's government and executed.

Aguinaldo withdrew his forces to Biak-na-Bato (Split Rock) in Bulacan province. From there he directed a harassing, guerilla-type warfare against the Spanish. Governor de Rivera wisely decided on negotiation. He arranged for a prominent lawyer, Dr. Pedro Paterno, to be the mediator. Paterno proved to be a patient negotiator. Finally on December 14, 1897, Aguinaldo signed the Pact of Biak-na-Bato. By the terms of this pact, Aguinaldo was to go into exile and a total of 1,700,000 pesos was to be paid by the Spanish as war indemnity. Aguinaldo received 600,000 pesos and left for Hong Kong, where he deposited the money to be used in a future fight against Spain. The balance was never paid by the Spanish government.

Some American historians feel that the revolutionary movement was at that point effectively finished and that Aguinaldo was simply bought off and would never have taken up the struggle again if the Americans had not entered the picture. This, however, is to overlook what was actually happening in the Philippines and Hong Kong. In the Philippines, the oppressive measures were intensified and sporadic armed clashes continued to occur. In Hong Kong a Patriotic

League was formed whose purpose was to get outside support for the revolutionary movement. Aguinaldo continued to exert his leadership and soon made contact with representatives of the American government. The history of the Philippines was now to enter a new phase, one quite unforeseen by Aguinaldo.

THE AMERICAN ACQUISITION (1898)

On the night of February 15, 1898, one-and-a-half months after Aguinaldo had arrived in Hong Kong, the United States battleship *Maine* was blown up in Havana Harbor. This triggered a series of events which led to the declaration of war by the United States against Spain on April 25, 1898. On this date, General Aguinaldo was in Singapore, having arrived there just four days before, and Admiral Dewey was in Hong Kong preparing to move against the Spanish Navy in Manila.

In Singapore, Aguinaldo was contacted by the American Consul, Pratt. Pratt indicated to him that the United States would appreciate his cooperation in the fight against Spain. He also quite innocently encouraged him to hope that the United States would in turn help him in his struggle for Philippine independence. For this Pratt was later reprimanded by the State Department.

Aguinaldo sailed back to Hong Kong. Before he arrived, Admiral Dewey had already sailed for Manila. Dewey later said, "I attached so little importance to Aguinaldo that I did not wait for him" (U.S. Senate 1902:Document 331, Part 3, 2927).

The story of the Battle of Manila Bay is familiar. May 1, early in the morning, Dewey and his fleet sailed past Corregidor. The Spanish Admiral Montojo and his fleet were waiting near Cavite — in shallow water in case any ships should be sunk! At 5:41 a.m. Admiral Dewey gave his command, "You may fire when you're ready, Gridley!" It was no contest. Before noon the Spanish fleet was sunk. American casualties were limited to one man who died of heat prostration.

On May 19, Aguinaldo and his staff returned to the Philippines on the *U.S.S. McCullouch*. His clear purpose was to take up again the revolution against Spain. He assumed, with every good reason, that the Americans would be his allies. The United States had clearly disclaimed any desire for territorial gain in the Cuban affair. President McKinley had said, "Forcible annexation by our code of morality would be criminal aggression" (quoted in Blount 1913:27). Senator Lodge had said:

> We are there [in Cuba] because we represent the spirit of liberty and the spirit of the new time, and Spain is over against us because she is medieval, cruel, dying. We have grasped no man's territory, we have taken no man's property, we have invaded no man's rights. We do not ask their lands (quoted in Blount 1913:27).

No wonder Aguinaldo told his people:

> Divine Providence is about to place independence within our reach. . . .

> Note that the Americans will attack by sea and prevent any reinforcements coming from Spain, therefore the insurgents must attack by land.

> You will, probably, have more than sufficient arms, because the Americans, having arms, will find means to help us. Wherever you see the American flag, there flock in numbers. They are our redeemers (quoted in Foreman 1906:483).

A tragedy of errors and misunderstandings now began to unfold. The Americans were woefully ignorant of the Philippines and what was happening there. As Laubach says, "There was everything to learn about the Filipino and almost nobody to do the teaching" (Laubach 1925:119). The Filipinos on their part were wonderfully naive about the ways of international politics. This was especially pointed out by the British observers, Foreman and Younghusband, who were well versed in the ways of imperialism.

At first Dewey seems to have considered Aguinaldo and his insurgents as bothersome but helpful. Volunteers were pouring into the insurgent army and, beginning in Cavite under Dewey's encouragement, they started to drive the Spanish back to Manila. Dewey said,

> I was waiting for troops to arrive, and I felt sure the Filipinos could not take Manila, and I thought that the closer they invested the city the easier it would be when our troops arrived to march in. It turned out as I expected, and we need not have lost a man (U.S. Senate 1902:Document 331, Part 3, 2936).

Meanwhile Aguinaldo consolidated his position of leadership by establishing a dictatorship on May 24, 1898. On June 12, 1898, now celebrated as Philippine Independence Day, Aguinaldo proclaimed independence, unfurling the Philippine flag. The government was changed from the dictatorship to the Revolutionary Government on June 23, 1898, with Aguinaldo as President.

It was during this series of events that Apolinario Mabini became the chief advisor of Aguinaldo. Mabini was a brilliant intellectual and political theorist who had been active in the Propaganda Movement. He had been stricken by paralysis in both legs, a defect which he keenly felt, but which may have saved him from Spanish persecution. He penned Aguinaldo's decrees, was his close advisor, and became the intellectual and moral leader of the revolutionary movement. It was no doubt because of the impressive results of his collaboration with Aguinaldo that Dewey wired Washington on June 23, 1898, the day of the proclamation of the Revolutionary Government, as follows:

> In my opinion these people are superior in intelligence and more capable of self-government than the natives of Cuba, and I am familiar with both races (quoted by Blount 1913:41).

American Army troops began arriving on June 30. General Merritt arrived in Cavite on July 25. By that time the Filipino army had Manila tightly surrounded. It seems that the Spaniards wanted to surrender to the Americans, not to the Filipinos, so that what is reported as a sham battle was arranged to satisfy Spanish honor. On August 13, 1898, the City of Manila fell to the Americans. The Filipino army was kept out by strict orders of General Merritt.

THE TREATY OF PARIS AND THE PHILIPPINE INSURRECTION OF 1899

By this time American intentions were beginning to be questioned by the Filipinos. It soon became obvious that the United States intended to take possession of the Philippines, at least temporarily. The reasons were several. First was the fact that the Spanish surrender had been made to the Americans. In Washington this meant that Philippine sovereignty was to be transferred to the United States by treaty. Too, there was a deep conviction in the minds of President McKinley and others that the Philippines simply was not prepared for self-government. There was definitely some justification for this feeling, but there was also mammoth ignorance on the part of many Americans concerning the true conditions in the Philippines. It is doubtful whether the Philippines was ready for an American-style democracy, but it might be asked whether this was required. Another reason for the American takeover was the interest of other foreign powers. Germany already had sent ships into Manila Harbor, bringing about a rather serious stand-off between Admiral Dewey and Vice-Admiral Van Diederichs, fortunately ending with the German withdrawal.

The general mood of the time cannot be overlooked. This was the "Manifest Destiny" era in United States history, and the prospect of an outpost in the Far East was very tempting. The philosophy of the "white man's burden" held sway. To educate and raise the civilization of backward peoples was the responsibility of the "advanced" nations. Related to this was the missionary motive. Wolff says:

> Formerly anti-war and generally anti-imperialist, the organized Protestant Church now descried another outlet for missionary activity. . . .

> Mr. McKinley and his wife, both ardent Methodists, did much to help the cause. "Do we need their consent," he asked, "to perform a great act for humanity?" And the Philippines were an even more worthy target than Cuba, for they were substantial in size and population and paved the way for God's work in China (1961:84-85).

One would take it that Mr. Wolff is not much in sympathy with these sentiments, but could it not be that after three centuries of Roman Catholic domination, Protestantism was the very thing that the Philippines needed? But, as a matter of fact, the missionary motive was not of decisive importance in the acquisition of the Philippines, and it is certainly to the credit of America's social conscience that vigorous opposition arose to what many felt to be imperialistic expansion. William Jennings Bryan, the Democratic party and the Anti-Imperialist League were especially vocal.

So the American negotiators pressed for the American acquisition of the Philippines in Paris. The Philippines was not represented nor was its special envoy, Agoncillo, listened to. On December 10, 1898, the Treaty of Paris was signed in which the Philippines, along with Puerto Rico and Guam, was ceded to the United States. The United

States in turn paid Spain the sum of $20,000,000. The treaty then came before the United States Senate to face a stormy debate before approval by a one-vote majority.

Meanwhile Aguinaldo and Mabini were not standing still. On September 15, 1898, the Congress of Malolos was called to draft a constitution. On January 23, 1899, almost two months after the signing of the Treaty of Paris, the first Philippine Republic was inaugurated, with General Aguinaldo as President. The Republic was never recognized by any foreign power, but it was recognized by the different areas of the Philippines, another indication that this was not simply a Tagalog affair.

The tension between the American forces and the Filipinos was near the breaking point. On February 4, 1899, a Filipino soldier refused to halt while trying to cross the San Juan Bridge. He was shot by the American sentry. Immediately hostilities began. It is not our purpose to tell the full story of this sad war. It is sufficient to say that although the outcome was never really in doubt, the war was a costly one. Its seriousness was constantly underestimated by the American commanders, especially General Otis. The fighting continued through 1899 into 1902. Effectively the war was over when Aguinaldo was captured through a ruse in which American officers posed as prisoners of war. Possibly American occupation of the Philippines was a necessity, but it would seem that had the early Filipino leaders been taken more seriously and treated with more respect, this war against the United States might have been avoided.

THE NEW CIVIL GOVERNMENT – BUILDING A NATION

This war, as all wars, was marked by abuses and atrocities on both sides. It could have had a disastrous effect on Philippine-American relations in general, and on American Protestant mission work in particular, but it did not. Why?

The answer must be found in America's colonial policy. Much to many Filipinos' surprise, America meant what she said about giving Filipinos an ever-increasing voice in their own government and establishing a rule of justice. After the tyrannical oppression of the Spaniards and the upheavals connected with the wars, the people were happy to live in peace again. Much credit should be given to the first civil governor of the Philippines, William H. Taft (1901-1904). Putting down banditry and outlawry, he established the base for a growing economy. He purchased the friar lands and began to distribute them, and established true religious liberty in the islands. The Filipino historian, Zaide, adds:

> Another great achievement of Taft was the winning of Filipino sympathy. His genial personality and his policy of "the Philippines for the Filipino" erased the hostility of the Filipinos to Uncle Sam and captivated their admiration and confidence (1958:250).

One of the most important contributions of the United States to the Philippines was their education system. Although the Spanish established a system of public schools in 1863, only under the Americans did the education of the masses really begin. On August 23, 1901, six hundred American teachers arrived on the Army transport *Thomas*. These "Thomasites," later followed by many others, scattered through the islands laying the foundation of a fine educational system. The English language was stressed, along with civics, history (especially American history), hygiene, sanitation and vocational arts.

Here, then, was a nation in transition. It had not gained independence as quickly as many had desired. Yet, by being turned in a new direction it was a stronger, better nation that finally achieved its goal in 1945, when in a spirit of peace and friendship, the American flag was lowered and the Philippine flag raised.

It was into this society in transition that Protestant Christianity was introduced, and within it that a religious revolution occurred. But before telling this story, we should first look a little more closely at this society which in many ways was so different from the society into which Roman Catholic Christianity had come more than three centuries earlier.

CHAPTER 6

EARLY TWENTIETH CENTURY
PHILIPPINES: A SOCIETY IN TRANSITION

The society into which Protestant Christianity came at the turn of the century presented quite a different picture than that of the sixteenth century when the Spanish arrived. For one thing it was much larger. According to the 1903 census, the total population was 7,635,426 — over ten times the estimated population of the islands in 1565. Of these, 6,987,686 were classified in the 1903 census as "civilized," 647,740 "wild," and of the latter probably more than two-fifths were Moros (Moslems) (U.S. Bureau of Census 1905:Vol. 2, 14). Updating the terminology we would say that 92 per cent of the people were Christianized lowlanders, about 3 per cent were Moslem tribal groups and 5 per cent were other pagan tribal groups.

Not only was it a larger society, but it was a more unified one. This refers specifically to the Christianized majority. The tribal minority seems to have changed very little culturally throughout the Spanish period. In the sixteenth century the Philippines was a congeries of Malayan tribal groups with a very fragmentary baranganic social structure. A few early American observers thought that this was still substantially the situation in 1900. Bishop Thoburn of the Methodist Episcopal Church, testifying before the Committee on the Philippines of the United States Senate in 1902, stated:

> The natives are very much, in many respects, like our American Indians, it strikes me. They have no cohesion among

themselves. Wherever I meet the Malays I find that they live to themselves; they go off in tribes and clans, and the biggest man is called a sultan and his jurisdiction is limited (U.S. Senate 1902:*Document* 331, Part 3, 2669).

This observation was made after a visit of only two weeks in 1899 and one week in 1900. During neither visit was he able to leave Manila. Bishop Thoburn was interpreting what he had seen in the light of his extensive experience among the Malayan peoples of Singapore and Malay Peninsula. He did, however, point up a significant characteristic of Malayan society — lack of cohesion — but seemed quite unaware of the tremendous changes brought about in Philippine society after over three centuries of Spanish rule. His statement is helpful for perspective, but dangerously misleading if allowed to stand alone.

In contrast, Governor Taft made this statement on the "Difference between Filipino and Other Malayan Races" in his testimony before the same committee:

> We feel this way about the people: They are unlike the Malay races, first, in that for three hundred years they have been educated in the Christian religion (U.S. Senate 1902: *Document* 331, Part 1, 342).

By the time of the Revolution in 1896 all the major lowland groups had become Hispanicized, so that there was a basic cultural unity between the various groups. It was quite justifiable to use the word "tribes" to refer to these groups when the Spanish arrived. But to speak of the "Christian tribes" in 1900 (as the 1903 census does) seems almost as out of place as to speak of the German, Irish and Italian tribes in the United States in the early 1900's. True, the Tagalogs, Ilocanos and Visayans were and are quite clannish. Yet it is clear that by the time of Rizal they were thinking of themselves as "Filipinos."

It is true that this Hispanicization did not involve the adoption of the Spanish language by the majority of the people. In 1903 less than 10 per cent of the people knew Spanish (U.S. Bureau of Census 1905:Vol. 2, 78). The native languages continued in strength. Having said this, one should not underestimate the importance of Spanish. It was the language of the educated minority who were the leaders. Rizal did most of his writing in Spanish, and it was his desire that the knowledge of Spanish should spread. Through the medium of Spanish the revolutionary leaders of one area could and did communicate with those of different areas. It was the *lingua franca* of the nation.

That Hispanicization of culture is not necessarily bound to the Spanish language is illustrated by the writings of the great nineteenth century Tagalog poet, Fransisco Balagtas (1788-1862). His epic poem, *Florante at Laura* ("Florante and Laura"), is a romance, but is also a subtle social protest against Spanish oppression. It is written in Tagalog, but contains many Hispanic literary allusions. Its cultural milieu is definitely European, not Malayan (Balagtas 1947).

Late nineteenth century Philippine society was a fascinating amalgam of the Hispanic and Malayan cultures. It was characterized by regionalism based on language and geography, yet with a growing sense of national unity.

THE FAMILY

The primary unit in Philippine society remained the family. The basic pattern of monogamous marriage was greatly strengthened by the Roman Catholic Church. The 1903 census reports that 33.1 per cent of the population were legally married — which in the Philippines meant married by the Church. Only 3.3 per cent were consensually married, contrasting strongly, the census says, with Cuba where only 15.7 per cent of the population were legally married (U.S. Bureau of Census 1905:Vol. 2, 69). This would indicate that the Catholic ideal of Christian marriage had been generally accepted. The position of women remained high. They were considered more responsible than the men. Foreman says:

> However, all over the Islands the women are more parsimonious than the men; but as a rule, they are more clever and discerning than the other sex, over whom they exercise great influence. Many of them are very dexterous business women and have made the fortunes of their families (1906:173).

Within the family there was a profound respect for elders — reinforced by discipline. Foreman also says that "the families are very united, and claims for help and protection are admitted however distant the relationship may be" (1906:170). The basic kindred structure of the pre-Spanish Malayan tribes thus persisted.

Marriage was arranged by the parents. The payment of dowry (*bigay-kaya*) was still practiced along with donation by the father of the bridegroom to defray the wedding expenses. Regarding residence after marriage, Foreman says:

> As a rule, the married couple live with the parents of one or the other, at least until the family inconveniently increases. In old age, the elder members of the families come under the protection of the younger ones quite as a matter of course. In any case, a newly-married pair seldom resides alone (1906:181).

In modern anthropological terminology, residence after marriage was ambilocal and the household usually included some relatives other than the nuclear family.

A completely new element that was brought into the family structure by the Spanish was the *compadre* system or "ritual co-parenthood" (Eggan 1956:424ff.). This describes the relationship between a parent and the person(s) whom he chooses to sponsor his child at baptism. Sometimes the person is chosen because of his wealth or influence. In this case the relationship tends to be merely formal. Often, however, the choice is a close friend and the affectional tie created is quite close. If the sponsor is a man he is subsequently addressed as *compadre* or *pare,* if a woman, *comadre* or *mare.* A Tagalog child addresses his sponsor as *ninong* (*ninang* if female) and he is known as *inanak.* This system effectively extends the family even wider than its already wide scope.

The family web has much meaning for the work of missions, as we shall see. Any effective evangelism must focus on this primary institution of Philippine society. Working against this structure predetermines slow growth. Working through the family web of relationships can bring gratifying results.

THE BARRIO AND TOWN

The Spanish program of *reducción,* working along with the *encomienda* system, as we have seen in Chapter 2, was aimed at breaking down the fragmentary structure and gathering the population into Spanish-type towns or *pueblos.* Although the Spanish worked on this for three centuries, they had only moderate success. Towns were established with the Church and the plaza in the center (see following map). The higher class were attracted to the towns, along with others, but underneath the old baranganic structure remained – with important modifications.

At first the Spanish recognized the leadership of the native *datus*. But, as Ruiz points out:

> In enforcing the authority of the *encomendero* the government took away the real power from the *datus* or chiefs by grouping the *barangays* into towns or *pueblos* and by making the *datus* headmen or *cabezas de barangays* who became mere tax collectors for the *encomenderos*. Obviously this led to the final absorption of the ancient Filipino land tenure (1942:33).

The *barangay* thus lost all governmental significance. The *datus* became the appointive tax collectors.

> The *barangay* was modified to become a territorial unit, a part of the *municipio* which was subdivision of a province somewhat intermediate between a U.S. county and a political township (Cutshall 1964:12).

At the turn of the century, however, the town did not loom large on the political landscape. The 1903 census lists only four towns which exceeded 10,000 and 31 whose population was between 5,000 and 10,000 in the town proper or *poblacion* (excluding Manila, which was in a class by itself). The four large towns were Laoag, Iloilo, Cebu and Nueva Cacera (Naga City today). In contrast, it counts 13,400 barrios with an average population of 500 each. The census goes on to explain that in fact in

> a number of cases the *poblacion* consists of a number of adjacent urban barrios and these have been added together to form the village or town, to which is given the name of the municipality (U.S. Bureau of Census 1905:Vol. 2, 35-36).

The 23 barrios of Cebu, which were urban and close together, were counted collectively as the city of Cebu. The *barangay* may not have survived as a political unit, but functionally it was reflected in the barrio.

The upper class Filipinos in each town made up the group of leaders known as the *principales* and from these the *gobernadorcillos* (heads of towns) and *cabezas de barangay* (heads of barrios) were chosen. These functioned under the direction of the parish priest and the Spanish officer of the local garrison. The main tasks of

FIGURE 3

MAP OF TOWN - BARRIO COMPLEX

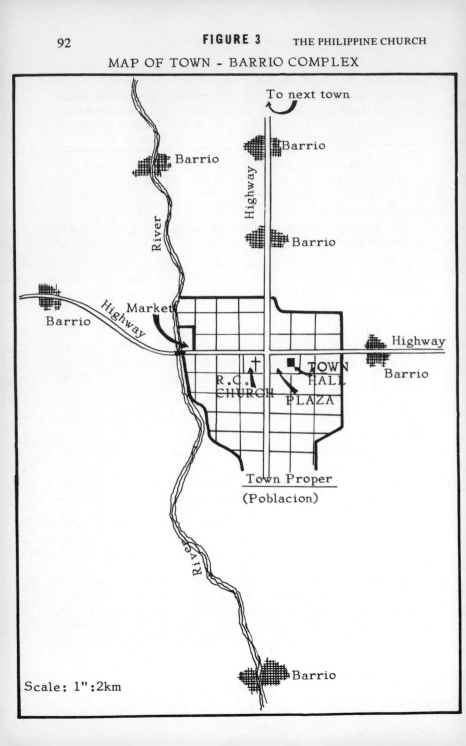

government on the local level were the collection of taxes and the maintenance of some local police protection. Otherwise the government was completely centralized. The parish priest resided in the town and could visit the barrio chapels (the old *visita* chapels) only on occasion. Of course, the friars could maintain tighter control of the barrios within the large expanses of the friar lands.

An even smaller geographical subdivision than the barrio was the *sitio*, or hamlet. This was not a governmental unit but referred to a small settlement which usually formed part of a barrio. Some local disputes could be settled informally in the *sitio,* but actual governmental structures began at the barrio level.

The population then was quite fragmented. The people thought of themselves as living in small groupings. Even geographically they were quite scattered — over 342 islands in 1903. Protestant missions, in seeking to reach this scattered and fragmented population, were faced with a tremendous task.

THE CITY

The city of Manila was unique. At the turn of the century it was *the* city of the Philippines. With its population of 219,928 it had no rival. It was the center of the commercial and political life of the nation. In a way it was the nation. Whoever controlled Manila controlled the Philippines. Since Manila was in the Tagalog area, some have tried to dismiss the revolution against Spain, which centered in Manila and its surrounding provinces, as a purely "Tagalog affair." But to dismiss the Revolution or anything else in this way is simply not to understand the importance of Manila in the life of the nation during that time.

The trade going through the Port of Manila, the extreme centralization of the Spanish government there, the colleges and hospitals — all these factors made it the center of national life. The process of urbanization had begun, and Manila would continue to grow in importance and influence. Manila had made Philippine nationalism possible, and there it would continue to flourish.

THE SOCIAL CLASSES

Philippine society at the end of the Spanish period was hierarchical, with a small, powerful upper class (10 per cent or less of the whole population) and a very much larger lower class.

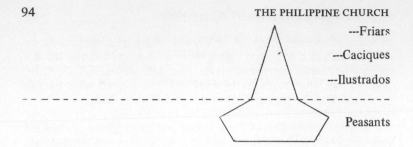

As is shown in the above diagram, the base of the society was the peasantry. Since the economy of the country was predominantly agriculture, these peasants were for the most part tenants of different types, but primarily share tenants. They were often referred to as the common *tao* (*tao* is the Tagalog word for "person" or "man"). Majul points out that there was neither a proletariat of industrial workers nor a well-developed bourgeoisie as existed in Europe, although there was a very small group of merchants in Manila — a beginning entrepreneurial class (1960:26, 27).

At the top of the social structure were the landowners. The richest and most powerful of these were the friars. The Filipino and Spanish landowners were known as *caciques*. This word originally came from Haiti, where it meant "chief." It came to take on a meaning somewhat like the word "boss," although the *cacique* would often wield the influence of a local chieftain. People of education were looked up to, even if they were not actually rich. These were the *ilustrados*, many of whom were landowners, *caciques*, yet some were not. The well-educated amounted to about 10 per cent of the population in 1903 (U.S. Bureau of Census 1905:Vol. 2, 15).

Dr. David P. Barrows, testifying before the Senate Committee on the Philippines, dwelt at some length on the social organization of the people (U.S. Senate 1902:*Document* 331, Part 1, 680-687). Dr. Barrows had gone to the Philippines to assist in organizing schools in the islands and then had become head of the Bureau of Non-Christian Tribes. Dr. Barrows began his testimony by explaining something of the pre-Spanish social structure of the Philippines, mentioning the *datu, maharlika,* semi-free and slave classes. He said he believed that "these two classes, a controlling dominant class [*gente ilustrados*] and an only partially free class [*gente baja*] have persisted to the present time." In speaking of the semi-free condition of many of the *gente baja,* Barrows was referring to their condition as share tenants who very often were in debt or peonage to the owners and thus were effectively bound to them. Significantly, Barrows felt that relations between the two classes were usually good, and that the peasants followed the dominant class.

(Ruiz [1942:78, 79] also refers to what he calls the problem of the attitudes and values of the *caciques* and the common *tao* toward each other. The *cacique* tended to be autocratic, overbearing, predatory but paternalistic. The common *tao,* on the other hand, exhibited a spirit of servility to his *cacique.*)

When asked about the feelings of the masses toward Americans, Dr. Barrows said they followed the dominant class closely. When the leaders became reconciled to the presence of the Americans, the resistance of the masses immediately ceased. This reinforces Nida's analysis that in this type of society, information and attitudes are transmitted from the top down and then out to the fringes. This had definite implications for the Christian mission in the Philippines when the early Protestant missionaries entered the islands. The active opposition of the *cacique* could make evangelism very difficult. On the other hand, the white American missionary would be identified with the *cacique* class by the common *tao.* This would have its advantages and disadvantages.

CHANGES UNDER EARLY AMERICAN RULE

Coming into the Philippines at a time of social upheaval, at a time of revolution, the Americans found the mass of Filipinos ready for a change — in fact, for many of them. Wernstedt and Spencer point up the most important of the changes:

> The long-run effect of American action, however, did much to both modernize and Americanize a Filipino society already occidentalized to a very considerable degree. Probably the most effective procedures were the installation of an efficient system of secularized, representative government administration, and the installation of a system of free national education. Gradually the first gave domestic self-rule, and the second produced an educated society with, finally, a working countrywide language among what had been a group of societies speaking many different languages and dialects. The American school teacher was the agent of cultural change

reaching far beyond the language instruction thus provided (1967:129).

The friars were removed soon after the American occupation. Then their lands were purchased and a conservative land tenure act was passed in order to distribute the land more equally. This removed at one stroke the primary cause of social unrest during the previous century. Unfortunately, however, the root causes were not removed. When the friars were removed, the power of the *caciques* was effectively increased. Ruiz has shown that through the years the lands that were sold under the new land laws tended to fall into the hands of fewer and fewer owners and that the Roman Church again built up its land holding (1942:47, 48). In fact, as the years went on, more and more friars returned — from other countries and from other orders — until today one-half of the total number of priests are regular priests, most of them foreign.

Thus many social problems remained unsolved. Nevertheless the Philippine economy took a tremendous leap forward with the coming of the Americans. Because of the free trade with the United States, the upper and middle classes came to enjoy a much higher standard of living. The middle class was indeed emerging. The eagerness of the people to learn English was amazing, and it soon replaced Spanish as the *lingua franca* of the islands.

Another layer of culture was being added. To the basic Malayan core and the deep layer of Hispanic culture was added a richly varied American contribution. The final product was still distinctly Filipino. Not the least important of the new additions was Protestant Christianity, brought by American missionaries who entered the Philippines almost immediately upon the American occupation of Manila. It is to that story that we now turn.

CHAPTER 7

THE INTRODUCTION AND GROWTH OF PROTESTANT CHRISTIANITY 1899-1946

The 333-year Roman Catholic encapsulation of the Philippines was shattered by the cannons of Admiral Dewey's battleships. To the credit of American Protestant Churches, this historic event did not pass unnoticed by their leaders. About two weeks after the Battle of Manila Bay, the Rev. George F. Pentecost rose in the Presbyterian General Assembly and with a colorful mixture of military and scriptural phrases said:

> We cannot ignore the fact that God has given into our hands, that is, into the hands of American Christians, the Philippine Islands, and there opened a wide door and effectual to their populations and has, by the very guns of our battleships, summoned us to go up and possess the land (quoted in Brown 1903:174).

On June 20, 1898, the Presbyterian Board began consultations with both the Baptist and Methodist Boards regarding the opening of a work in the Philippines. On November 21, 1898, it appointed the Rev. and Mrs. James B. Rodgers, then newly returned missionaries to Brazil, to become the first duly appointed missionaries to the Philippines. Meanwhile, although the Baptists and Methodists had informed the Presbyterians that they would not be able to enter the Philippines immediately, both were very concerned and took steps which soon led to the sending of missionaries from these two boards as well.

These were the days of Protestant "firsts" in the Philippines:

1. The first Protestant service in the islands was conducted by YMCA secretaries Glunz and Jackson on August 14, 1898.

2. The first agent of the British and Foreign Bible Society who was allowed to enter the Philippines with a supply of Bibles and Gospel portions was Mr. Charles B. Randall. He arrived on September 6, 1898. Brown mentions another agent, Mr. Bartter, who arrived soon after the landing of American troops, but gives no date (1903:186).

3. In November, 1898, Randall, accompanied by Glunz and Jackson and another minister, made a trip to Pangasinan to distribute Gospel portions.

4. Bishop James M. Thoburn, missionary Bishop for the Methodist Church in Southern Asia, visited Manila in March, 1899, and held a week of evangelistic meetings at the *Teatro Filipino* for American service personnel. It was a time of great tension, for fighting had just broken out between the American and Filipino forces. Bishop Thoburn was assisted by Mr. Arthur Prautch, who had worked under Thoburn in India, but was now an exporter in Manila. Prautch was licensed as a local preacher and followed up the American converts who were organized into Methodist classes.

5. The Rev. James B. Rodgers made his way to the Philippines from Brazil. Hearing of the fighting around Manila he left his family in Hong Kong and arrived in Manila alone on April 21, 1899 – the first regularly appointed missionary to arrive in the Philippines.

6. Three weeks later, on May 7, 1899, Rodgers held his first service in the home of a Mr. Poblete. The sermon was in Spanish, liberally sprinkled with Portuguese words. Seven attended this service.

7. The first Filipinos were baptized by Mr. Rodgers on October 22, 1899.

Mr. Rodgers' first service was attended by only seven Filipinos and four of them were members of one family: Mr. Paulino Zamora and his three sons, Nicolas, Ricardo and Jesus. This family looms large in the story of Protestant beginnings in the islands, underlining the role of key families in the expansion of Christianity. Their story is an important one, for it illustrates the providential preparation for the acceptance and propagation of the Gospel which we meet over and over again in the history of missions.

Mr. Paulino Zamora was the nephew of Father Jacinto Zamora,

one of the three Filipino priest martyrs of 1872. This execution must have had the same effect on Paulino Zamora as it had on Rizal, for he too became an enemy of the friars. He obtained a Bible from a ship's captain and may have had some contact with the Bible Society agents Lallave and Castells in the tragedy of 1889, when, soon after entering the islands, Lallave, a former priest, died under suspicious circumstances, and Castells was quickly deported. Zamora became very interested in the Bible, and for this he was imprisoned and later exiled to a prison colony. He was not released until the signing of the Treaty of Paris in December, 1898. He then made his way back to the Philippines and, as we have seen, was soon in contact with the Protestant missionaries.

From this point on the story becomes increasingly complex as other missions begin their work. The first permanent Methodist missionary arrived in March, 1900, the first Baptist in May, 1900. United Brethren and Protestant Episcopal missionaries began to arrive in 1901. It is not our purpose to give the complete history of Protestant missions in the Philippines. Rather, we will take two groups, the Methodists and the Baptists, who have different patterns of growth, and consider their work in some detail. But before proceeding to these case studies, we need to mention the significant spirit of cooperation among these early Protestant missions which found expression in the Evangelical Union, formed in 1901.

From the very beginning it was the Presbyterian mission which showed special concern that Protestant mission work in the Philippines be conducted in a brotherly spirit of cooperation and non-competitiveness. We have already seen how the Presbyterian Board conferred with the others before deciding definitely to launch their Philippine mission. The same spirit showed itself on the field on April 24-26, 1901, when a meeting of all Protestant missionaries convened in Manila to discuss the formation of an Evangelical Union. Attending the meeting were representatives of the Presbyterian, Methodist, United Brethren, Christian and Missionary Alliance Missions, and the YMCA and Bible Societies. The Baptists were not present, but immediately ratified the agreement. The Protestant Episcopal Mission refrained from joining, possibly because they had already decided not to work among the Roman Catholic population of the islands.

At this meeting the Evangelical Union of the Philippine Islands was formed. Article II of the constitution states the object of the organization:

> Article II — Object. It shall be the object of this society to unite all the evangelical forces in the Philippine Islands for the purpose of securing comity and effectiveness in their missionary operations (Brown 1903:188).

Two very important decisions were made. First, "the name 'Iglesia Evangélica' shall be used for the Filipino Churches which shall be raised up" — with the denominational name in parenthesis, if needed. Secondly,

> that each Mission now represented on the field accept the responsibility for the evangelization of certain well-defined areas, to be mutually agreed upon (Brown 1903:190).

Thus a strict comity arrangement was entered into by the various boards which was recognized until the end of the Second World War. Although denominational differences were not easily obscured, even with the adoption of a common name, the agreement no doubt was a prime factor in the eventual formation of the United Church of Christ in the Philippines. In this first generation of Protestant missions in the Philippines, comity enabled Protestant Christianity to spread throughout the islands with a minimum of friction.

The record of cooperation in the Philippines is indeed so notable that one hardly dares make any negative comment. However, to give balance to the picture some observations may be allowed. Under comity it was inevitable that the churches that sprang up in the different mission areas took on a distinctive character in each area. This had its good and bad points. Lack of cross-fertilization and of constructive competition can result in a spirit of self-complacency. Churches can and sometimes did stress cooperation and ecumenism to the neglect of the more important task of continuing evangelism. Comity, then, was good in its time, but it may not be a tragedy that it is no longer observed.

THE METHODIST CHURCH

The story of Methodism in the Philippines begins with the vision of a great missionary bishop of the Methodist Church — Bishop James M. Thoburn. Bishop Thoburn believed very strongly in the

43975

personal leading of God. He had first felt God's leading to India. From India he felt led to Burma, then to Singapore. While serving in Singapore he began to feel a special interest in the islands to the east — the Philippines. When the cable came to proceed to Manila and carefully examine the situation there, he was eager to go. He arrived for this first visit on February 28, 1899, and stayed for two weeks with the results that we have already noted (page 98).

The meetings at the theater were continued by Mr. Prautch and Chaplain Stull. In June, at the request of some Filipino Masons, the meetings were opened to Filipinos, with Chaplain Stull preaching in English and being interpreted into Spanish. At one of these meetings the interpreter did not come. The elderly Paulino Zamora, whom we have met before at Mr. Rodgers' first service, stood and introduced himself as a Protestant. Mr. Prautch invited him to preach. He declined, but offered the services of his son Nicolas. Nicolas Zamora's message was warmly received, and he was asked to continue his ministry with them.

In February, 1900, the first missionaries of the Methodist Church arrived — three single ladies, one a doctor. These began a work in Manila, but were soon transferred to India and Singapore. The first evangelistic missionaries arrived shortly after. In March, Bishop Thoburn returned for one week. During this visit he took the very significant step of ordaining Nicolas Zamora, who thus became the first ordained Filipino Protestant minister.

The first District Conference of the Philippine Islands Mission, August 20, 1900, reported the following statistics (Deats 1964:8):

> 7 preaching places for Filipino work
> 8 weekly services
> 220 probationers
> 7 baptisms
> 7 native workers
> 38 marriages

Looking at these figures one is tempted to ask whether it was easier to get married than baptized! The recruitment of national workers at this early period was notable, not only among the Methodists, but among other missions as well. Some object to the use of paid national evangelists as being against good indigenous church-planting principles. But even Nevius had his paid national supervisors, and it is doubtful whether the Methodists in the Philippines could have achieved their early great growth without using paid nationals. It is important to add that the early reports emphasize that the growth was rapid enough that there were more unpaid than paid workers in those early days.

Nicolas Zamora and his helpers multiplied services in and around Manila. Most of these were held in the homes of interested persons who gathered their own small congregations. The first Methodist church building was dedicated by Bishop Warne on August 12, 1900, in Pandacan, Manila. It was a simple, thatched-roof structure. When the congregation bought its first piece of land, they found that there was no law by which a non-Catholic could secure title to real estate. Methodist supervisor Stuntz went directly to Governor Taft, who

> without consulting a book or so much as moving his chair, touched a bell, summoned his secretary, dictated a law in three sections covering the whole case and in 15 minutes it was typescript before him. . . . He said that it was the intention of the Committee and himself to remove all disabilities from the Protestants just as soon as their existence was brought to their attention (World Wide Mission, Jan. 1902; *quoted in* Hollister 1956:225).

As the early Spanish friars had benefited from the presence of Spanish civil power, so now early Protestant missionaries found an ally in the American civil government. The difference was that Governor Taft was here implementing the principle of religious liberty, not actively promoting one religion at the expense (or to the exclusion) of another.

As the people of the Manila area came to accept American control and began to enjoy some of the benefits, the responsiveness of the people to the Gospel greatly increased. In 1902 Bishop Thoburn testified before the United States Senate Committee on the Philippines:

> We cannot furnish preachers enough to preach to the audiences who wish to hear our preaching, we cannot half meet the demand. When I was there at first it would have been difficult to have collected an audience of 100. Now we are preaching to 12,000 people in Manila and vicinity every Sunday. Then in the provinces outside we cannot meet the

demand at all, nor can we meet the demands for schools (U.S. Senate 1902:*Document* 331, Part 3, 2690).

Growth was rapid. Evangelism and church planting were emphasized. In 1903, forty regularly organized congregations were reported. Laymen played an important role in this expansion, with each congregation having from one to five "exhorters" (lay workers) and local preachers. There were only four missionaries and five paid Filipino workers at this time (Deats 1964:12).

Some areas proved more responsive than others. The town of Mexico, Pampanga, is an example of a responsive town. In 1904, the president (*gobernadorcillo*) of the town and a majority of the town council were Methodists. There were 400 members in the town, and Deats adds the important bit of information that in one barrio, Panipuan, all the families but one were Methodists (1964:13). We are given no information as to how this occurred. However, it does point up an important, recurring pattern in Protestant work in the Philippines. Every town has a number of barrios, maybe ten, possibly as many as fifty. When a movement to Christ occurs, it is most often in one or several of these barrios. It does not sweep the whole town generally, but moves through responsive barrios while bypassing others. We have already seen that the barrio is a more basic unit in Philippine society than the town, and the way in which the Church grows in the barrios must be carefully studied.

Stuntz reports in 1904 a total membership of 6,842 with ten missionaries, comparing this with the Presbyterian membership of 1,000 with 14 missionaries. However, it should be noted that these figures are not strictly comparable. The Methodists give as their total membership the combined totals of the full members and the probationary members, while the Presbyterian figure is communicant membership. Nevertheless, the Methodist growth is notable. Stuntz says, "Such ripeness for evangelism has never been seen in any Roman Catholic field" (1904b:492). He adds the illuminating statement that "A most gratifying feature of the work is its spontaneity. We have never begun work in a city until we had been invited there" (1904a:392). He then gives an example of what Roland Allen would refer to as the spontaneous expansion of the Church.

The example is that of the church in Malolos, the provincial capital of Bulacan. The work developed in the following way.

1. The missionary and the believers prayed for an opening in Malolos for months.

2. Mr. Goodell, the missionary, was told of a widow, Mrs. Estrella, who was ready to have Protestant services in her house. She had heard Zamora preach in Tondo. When Goodell arrived there he was welcomed as "an angel of God."

3. Regular services began at once in the barrio of Atlag.

4. Within five months the church had a membership of 185.

5. A church building was built seating 200. Fifty dollars was contributed from the Church Extension Fund.

6. Before the building was ready for use, people eight miles away were converted in the "house-to-house services." (Were there any family links with the church in the first town? This kind of information unfortunately is not given.)

7. In less than three months the membership in the second town was larger than in the first.

8. Within one year this second church "swarmed off" (Stuntz' term), and the most flourishing church of all grew up — with little help from the missionary.

Now we can gain some insight into Methodist church-planting method. Some important things are not told us, but note the following from what is told.

1. The missionary had a definite plan of outreach. He was praying that he could get into Malolos.

2. He wisely waited for an invitation so that when he entered there would be someone there who was sympathetic to him and to his message. He was trying to follow the natural lines of communication.

3. The gathering of the church began immediately as people accepted the message.

4. The growth was rapid enough that a chapel could be built with only a little help from Manila.

5. The evangelistic program included a definite outreach into the surrounding barrios and towns (note the "house-to-house" services). Was this done in a random manner or were natural relationships such as kinship used as bridges?

6. The process of "hiving off" or "swarming off" must have been encouraged, as it happened twice within a year and a half.

7. Church multiplication was not made dependent upon missionary presence and help. Spontaneous expansion was encouraged.

8. The relatively large numbers would indicate that the people were moving in groups — at least as families. This would minimize the problems of individual conversions against the pressures of the social group.

But many questions remain. For example, were these converts Roman Catholics or Aglipayans? What classes were involved? Why did this enormous initial growth slow down? How much opposition was encountered?

The Zamora Schism

As the Church grew, problems arose. Nationalistic feelings did not remain long buried. Nationalism, we should remember, is not a purely post-World War II phenomenon. It has been a strong force in Philippine Church life since the Revolution of 1896. It was, as we shall see, the motivating force which led to the formation of the Independent Philippine Church. It early showed its strength in the Methodist Church, as well.

Nicolas Zamora and his zealous Filipino fellow workers contributed greatly to the early growth of Philippine Methodism. Understandably, these men wanted to have a significant voice in the affairs of their Church. In addition they were politically nationalistic; that is, they desired Philippine independence and were resentful of American domination. News of the 1902 Senate hearings reached the Philippines, and we can be sure that the testimony of Methodist Bishop Thoburn on the inability of Filipinos to rule themselves was not favorably received. Too, there were personal differences between Zamora and some of the missionaries. During the years 1904-1909 the tension increased until on February 28, 1909, at St. Paul's Methodist Church, Tondo, Manila, Zamora announced the formation of the independent La Iglesia Evangelica Metodista en las Islas Filipinas, or IEMELIF, as it is commonly known. This Church has become the largest completely indigenous Evangelical Church in the Philippines. Today its membership is about 25,000. It is significant that this division had very little effect on the rate of growth of the Methodist Church. Church leaders fear schism, but a growing, aggressive Church has much less to fear than a stagnated Church.

The Methodist Graph of Growth

The primary tool of church growth research is the graph of

growth on the particular Church being studied. Before proceeding to analyze the Methodist graph of growth, a brief word of explanation is needed. Why is the graph of growth so helpful? The answer is that by placing the year-by-year membership statistics of a Church on a graph, we are able to get immediately a picture of its growth history. We are particularly interested in identifying both the periods of rapid growth and the periods of slowdown or decline. The accuracy of the picture naturally depends upon the accuracy of the available statistics. In the case of the Methodist Church in the Philippines we are fortunate to have an entire thesis devoted to a detailed study of Methodist statistics in the Philippines (Bibay 1965). Unfortunately, Bibay concluded that Methodist statistics are "not always correct, not consistent and not understandable" (1965:183). However, despite the many statistical and reporting problems he encountered, Bibay was able to give us a usable set of statistics from which we have constructed our graph. But while interpreting this graph we must always be aware of the statistical problems which underlie it.

Nevertheless the graph is instructive. We see the early rapid growth of full membership from nothing in 1900 to 16,569 in 1908. The graph then appears to flatten out for several years, though exact statistics for 1909-1911 are not available. This slowdown may have been due to the Zamorista split, which occurred in 1909. However, there is no sharp decline, so possibly the memberships of the schismatic churches were included in the total figures for a while.

The period of very rapid early growth ended in 1908. Between 1908 and 1935 there was a definite slowdown in the rate of growth. Why the slowdown? Several reasons are probable. First, the initial responsiveness of the general population had passed. Revitalization of the Roman Catholic Church in the Philippines was beginning to be effective. During much of this period the attention of the Protestant Churches was focused on the problems of Christian unity and ecumenism. Philippine Methodism interacted uncertainly with the movement which finally led to the formation of the United Church of Christ in the Philippines. (This matter was extensively discussed at the 1934 Annual Conference.) The Depression of 1929 also took its toll. The small dip in the graph in 1934 is probably due to the second schism, which occurred over a matter of discipline (also with some nationalistic overtones) and which led to the formation of the independent Philippine Methodist Church, which later united with the United Church of Christ.

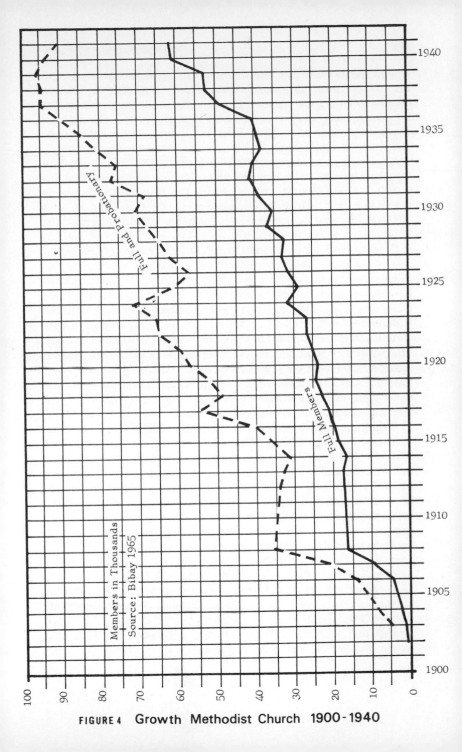

FIGURE 4 Growth Methodist Church 1900-1940

Members in Thousands
Source: Bibay 1965

Full and Probationary

Full Members

The relationship between the total (full plus probationary) and the full membership curve should give an indication of the effectiveness of the "perfecting" or nurturing ministry of the Church. Shearer (1966:52) discusses the problem of the ratio of *community* (the total number of adherents) and *communicants* (adult baptized believers). He points out that a large community-to-communicant ratio is related to inadequate Christian nurture. This problem, by the way, is especially acute in the Roman Catholic Church in the Philippines. The case of the Methodists was not so severe, but the growing separation of the two lines on the graph after 1914 should have been a matter of concern to the leaders of the Church.

Even when rapid growth was apparently resumed in 1937, all was not well. The statistics themselves are somewhat suspect, for this sudden jump occurs during the year when the Church was divided into two separate Annual Conferences. Even if the statistics are accepted at face value, another problem is encountered in the 1939 Philippine Island Annual Conference Report (as distinguished now from the North Philippine Annual Conference of Northern Luzon). This Annual Conference reported a full membership of 30,945, 7,526 of whom were listed as inactive. One-half of the entire third district (Bulacan) was listed as inactive. Later we shall see that the Methodists dropped this category altogether, for it is almost meaningless to continue to count those who are not active members, especially since many of them cannot even be found.

These problems of growth which have been pointed up by the study of the growth graph should not be allowed to obscure the fact that the Methodist Church was the leading Protestant Church in pre-war Philippines, consistently larger than any other denomination. Of all the Churches that entered at the turn of the century, they alone showed growth that was actually commensurate with the responsiveness of the people during the early period. Devotion to evangelism and church planting bore fruit.

THE BAPTISTS

Turning now to the history of the Baptist mission in the Philippines, we note again God's providential preparation for the opening of the work.

The story begins in Spain. The Rev. Eric Lund, a Swedish Baptist working under the American Baptist Missionary Union, had been conducting a mission for seamen in Barcelona since 1877. Thus he was in Barcelona during the entire period of the Philippine Propaganda Movement which centered in that city. He may have been aware of the expatriate Filipino community, and of the newspaper *La Solidaridad*. Fidel de P. Castells, one of the two early (1899) Bible Society agents, whose work was so tragically cut short (see page 99), was one of Lund's early converts (Sitoy 1967:52). This would indicate an early interest in the Philippines on the part of Mr. Lund. In 1898 a young Filipino, a native of Capiz and a Visayan, was converted under Lund. He was Braulio Manikan, formerly a student for the priesthood. This young man began to teach Mr. Lund the Ilongo (a Visayan dialect) while Mr. Lund taught him the Scriptures. Translation of the Gospels was begun and a printing of them was made in Spain. Yet another Visayan, Adriano Osorio y Reyes, was converted in Spain. He later joined the Presbyterian work in Iloilo. Rodgers refers to him as "a tower of strength for many years, journeying all over the field . . ." (1940:72).

It is no surprise, then, that the American Baptists turned to Mr. Lund to open their work in the Philippines. Manikan accompanied Lund to assist him in establishing the Baptist mission in the islands and to continue to help in the translation work. They sailed from Barcelona on March 24, 1900, and on April 26 they arrived in Manila. The following Sunday Lund preached in the Presbyterian church to a "fair sized congregation" (Lund 1900:526). On May 1 they were in Iloilo. Lund was convinced that the Baptist head-quarters should be in the Iloilo vicinity. The Presbyterians had already begun work in Iloilo proper, so the Baptists began in the twin town of Jaro. This raised a problem of comity that was not finally settled until 1925, when the Presbyterians turned over their work in Iloilo to the Baptists.

Rodgers (1940) reports that in the beginning of the work there was considerable anti-American feeling, but that the attitude of the people quickly changed. This anti-American feeling does not seem to have been general, however, even in the early days. Briggs says that the first missionary who preached in western Negros in 1900 was welcomed by a great representative mass meeting of the leaders of the "Negros Republic." People there declared that soon the entire island would be Protestant (Briggs 1913:111-112). It is significant that this was before American sovereignty was firmly established in the islands.

Mr. Lund continued with his work of translation of the Scriptures, spending the mornings in this work. He was soon joined by Briggs and others in evangelistic work, and by Dr. Lerrigo, who began medical work. Health seems to have been a particularly serious problem in these early days, with several emergency furloughs frustrating the extension of the work.

There was much Roman Catholic opposition in Jaro in those early days. Jaro, the town which the missionaries had chosen as their headquarters, was also the seat of the archbishop. The persecution finally became so intense that the life of Placido Matta, one of Lund's helpers in his Bible translation work, was threatened. He paid no attention to the threat, and one morning as he was walking to Iloilo, he was hacked to death by bolos wielded by four assailants — a martyr to his faith. Later, one of the assailants was converted because of the Christian bravery which he had witnessed.

Nevertheless, the missionaries were greatly encouraged. The translation of the New Testament into Ilongo was completed and printed at Baptist expense (since it was a "Baptist" version, translating the word "baptize" by the word for "immerse"). Evangelism met with great responsiveness, particularly in the barrios. In a 1906 report, Briggs explains the shift of emphasis from the town to the barrio:

> Our plan, on first coming to the Visayan Islands, was to evangelize the towns, as nothing was known of these barrio peasants. The towns, however, steeped in vices and Romanism, refused to be evangelized, while the barrios, even before plans were made for receiving them, accepted the gospel, having been for decades wonderfully prepared for its coming. I have come heartily and enthusiastically to believe that these barrio peasants are the key to the religious situation, and we thank God that in leading us into the barrios he has given us not them only, but the whole people. Here, as in other countries, the inevitable trend is from the country into the city, from the barrio into the town. In evangelizing the barrios we reach the Visayan race at its source. How wonderfully God foresaw all and prepared the way for the salvation of this whole people!
>
> There are possibly more than 25,000 souls living in the barrios in my district. Probably our present Baptist constituency

numbers more than 10,000, of whom some 2,500 have been baptized . . . (A.B.M.U. Annual Report 1906:369).

The responsiveness of central Panay Island is shown in the Panayan Petition. In 1901, the Baptist Missionary Union in Boston received a petition from more than seven thousand Filipinos in one particular district of Panay asking for a missionary to come and work among them. The opening of this petition read as follows:

List of people of this company, subject to this town of Janiway, with names and appellations:

Head men	35
Aged and sick	310
Working men	1,466
Women liable to pay taxes	1,937
Young people	4,304
Total	7,934 (sic)

(The Baptist Missionary Magazine, September, 1901:601)

These people lived in seven barrios around the town of Janiway. Unfortunately, Lund became very ill (with dysentery?), so he forwarded this petition to the home office and then left for Spain for an emergency medical furlough. Briggs had just recently arrived on the field, but the invitation apparently could not immediately be accepted. The sincerity of this invitation is shown by the continued openness of the group to the Gospel in spite of persecution and the 1902 cholera epidemic, which was blamed on the Protestants. They frequently sent messengers to Jaro, to keep in contact with the missionaries. In 1906 Briggs reported:

I have had the great privilege of baptizing more than 1,000 disciples, most of whom have been Protestants for three or four years. . . . The great movement among the peasants in Panay, in 1901, is now a greater and more significant reality than it was then. The only reason why we have not 10,000 or 15,000 baptized believers in that district today is that our forces here have never been sufficient to enable us to reach the people, baptize them, and arrange for their further instruction (*Missionary Review of the World,* May 1905:399).

Here was the beginning of a small-scale people movement of the type that could be expected in the Philippines. The underlying fragmented baranganic social structure which we have described is conducive to this type of people movement. A group of barrios and towns in a specific geographical area within a single language area were responsive, and the group dynamics of a people movement were beginning to operate. The tragedy was that it was not followed through as thoroughly as it should have been. In this situation we cannot help but feel that the sending Church was more responsible for the failure to harvest than the missionaries. The great personal sacrifices of the early Baptist missionaries, especially in the matter of health, did not seem to have met with the responses of encouragement and reinforcements that should have been forthcoming from the home churches.

However, something more must be said, for this is a recurring problem. People movements and wide responsiveness often occur unannounced and usually face a shortage of workers. What should a Church or mission do when confronted by this kind of situation? First, workers from less responsive fields should be moved into the responsive area. The Baptists made a small move of this type when they transferred Lund from Spain to the Philippines. Second, and more important, national leaders of the people themselves must be won, speedily trained and mobilized for church growth. In this mobilization of national leadership, both ministerial and lay, the Methodists were much more effective than any other group in the Philippines. Their great growth was probably largely due to this fact. Admittedly, it is very difficult to compare the Methodist work and the Baptist work because of the great difference in the areas given each under comity, and we must be careful of making judgments at this distance in time. Yet it would seem that the Baptist missionaries may not have utilized local leadership to the extent they should have. As long as church multiplication is tied closely to the presence of the missionary, great growth is less likely.

When we move into the second decade of the century, the Baptists give us a classical case study of consolidation displacing extension, a perennial temptation in missions. In the annual report of 1913, we read the following note:

> Following the published policy of the Foreign Mission Society not to enter upon any new work until the present occupied fields are more thoroughly manned and equipped, the Philippine Islands mission voted not to enter the Island of Samar,

lying to the east of Panay, leaving it entirely to other
denominational missions. Intensive development is desired.
For this in the evangelistic department it was estimated that
the present force is sufficient for the next period of five years
(1913:123).

In its practical outworking, consolidation meant emphasis upon
education. The industrial school begun in Jaro in 1906 was
developed into Central Philippine College, which has since grown
into the noted Central Philippine University. In addition, high
schools (academies) were established in many towns of Panay and
Negros. The early annual reports all began with the section on
"Evangelism." But in 1916, for example, the evangelism report was
placed last, the longer educational report first. The missionaries
no doubt felt that this was what they should do for the good of the
Church, but this move towards "consolidation" seriously decreased
the rate of growth. No new stations were reported until 1928. It is
one thing to be forced to slow down by difficult circumstances, but
it is quite another to accept this as good mission strategy. This is not
to criticize the educational program itself, however, for the schools
which were established during this period produced a generation of
educated Christian leaders who sparked the postwar Baptist growth,
especially in West Negros.

The Baptist Graph of Growth

Looking at the graph, we note that the work which had begun in
1900 had reached only 500 in 1903. Growth in this measure must be
judged slow in view of the evident responsiveness of the area, but
this slow growth was due in part to severe health problems and
personnel shortage. The membership then picked up, doubling the
next year, and nearly doing so again the following year, reaching a
total of 2,403 in 1906. The decadal growth between the years 1904
and 1908 was 166 per cent. The rate of growth then decreases and
between the years 1908 and 1924 the decadal growth is 50 per cent.
On some fields this could be considered very good growth, yet in
this case, because of the responsiveness and in the light of the
conscious policy of consolidation, this must be judged slow growth.
In 1924 the graph swings wildly upward and oscillates for a few
years before settling down to the 9,000 – 10,000 membership level.
This rapid growth does not appear to be due to a sudden rise in

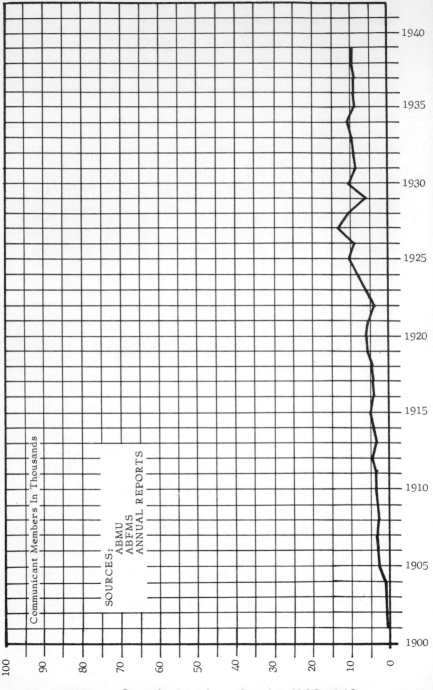

Communicant Members In Thousands

SOURCES:
ABMU
ABFMS
ANNUAL REPORTS

1940
1935
1930
1925
1920
1915
1910
1905
1900

100 90 80 70 60 50 40 30 20 10 0

FIGURE 5   Growth American Baptist 1900-1940

evangelistic activity, although there does seem to have been more action in this area. Instead, this is *transfer* growth. In 1925, the Presbyterians formally turned over their work in Iloilo to the Baptists. There seems to have been some uncertainty on the part of some local churches as to which denomination they would be associated with. This may explain the wild fluctuations in the graph between the years 1924 and 1932. The growth curve now definitely plateaus and does not begin its upward swing again until after 1927, when a schism occurred and the theologically conservative Association of Baptists for World Evangelism was formed. This may help explain the lack of growth during this latter part of the prewar period.

It is hard to feel that the growth of the Baptists was in any way commensurate with the responsiveness of the Ilongo population among whom they worked. Throughout this period of theological uncertainty and financial difficulty at home, the sending mission was not prepared to plan aggressively for great growth. It is small wonder that the missionaries could not keep up the great vision of early men like Briggs, and became satisfied with little growth, when great growth was possible.

THE PHILIPPINE INDEPENDENT CHURCH

Our description of this period must include a brief discussion of the very significant Philippine Independent Church, which arose simultaneously with the introduction of Protestant Christianity and grew quickly to become a much larger movement. This Church contrasts with the Protestant Churches in that it was not introduced from without by foreigners, but arose as a truly Filipino movement with indigenous leadership. It was first known by its Spanish title — La Iglesia Filipina Independiente (I.F.I.).

Historical writings about this Church are extraordinarily marked by bias — friendly, suspicious or antagonistic. To find an objective account seems impossible. The one work that makes extensive use of primary sources and archival materials is the two-volume work *Revolution in the Philippines* (1961:Vol. 1; 1965:Vol. 2) by Achutegui and Bernad. Unfortunately, the religious bias of these Jesuit scholars is so apparent that it colors all of their conclusions. Nevertheless, their careful historical research stands in contrast to the more popular, less carefully done books such as that of the

Episcopalian Whittemore, *Struggle For Freedom* (1961). A scholarly, objective account has yet to be written.

The founder of this Church was Gregorio Aglipay (hence it is sometimes called the "Aglipayan Church"). He was born on or about May 5, 1860 (even the date of his birth is debated!), in Batac, Ilocos Norte. His place of birth is significant, as this Church has been strongly Ilocano. Its leadership has been predominantly Ilocano, and even today it has more members (over one-tenth of the total) in Ilocos Norte than in any other province. Aglipay grew up during the same period as Rizal, and probably attended Santo Tomás University when Rizal was studying there. We can only conjecture that he came under some of the same nationalistic influences as Rizal. Aglipay prepared for the priesthood at Vigan and was ordained in 1889. Between 1890 and 1898 he served in a number of parishes. He seems to have had some contact with the Revolution before the Americans arrived, but appears to have been somewhat torn in his loyalties. After Dewey's victory in May, 1898, Aglipay was sent on a mission by Archbishop Nozaleda of Manila to General Makabulos of the insurgents (Aguinaldo had not yet returned) to encourage him to join forces with the Spaniards against the Americans. The mission was unsuccessful, but Aglipay did come in contact with the leaders of the Revolution, Aguinaldo and Mabini, upon their return. Aglipay was persuaded to throw in his lot with the revolutionaries.

Now began the series of ecclesiastical maneuvers which were soon to lead to the excommunication of Aglipay and later to the founding of the Independent Church. In order to understand these actions, we must realize that Aglipay believed strongly that the Philippines would gain its independence under Aguinaldo. While the Americans acted as if the Revolutionary Government did not exist, Aglipay acted in firm conviction as to the authority and rightness of that government. Because Manila had been taken by the Americans and the rest of the Philippines was under Aguinaldo's control, the revolutionary leaders felt that the Spanish hierarchy's control of the Philippine Church under Archbishop Nozaleda was now invalid. Mabini put it this way: The Spanish bishops possessed their authority from the fact that the Spanish Government had presented them to the Vatican for appointment; hence, with the collapse of Spanish sovereignty, the bishops also fell (Achutegui and Bernad 1961:Vol. 1, 105).

On this basis, Aguinaldo appointed Aglipay *Vicario General Castrence* (Military Vicar General) on October 20, 1898. Aguinaldo's next step was to have himself appointed Ecclesiastical Governor of Nueva Segovia, which comprised all of northern Luzon. He obtained this appointment from Bishop Campomanes, a Dominican friar imprisoned by the revolutionary government. This brought down the ire of the Spanish hierarchy, and Aglipay was excommunicated by Archbishop Nozaleda.

Mabini and Aglipay argued that this excommunication by a bishop who in reality had lost his see was invalid. On October 23, 1899, an ecclesiastical assembly was called at Paniqui, Tarlac, the purpose of which was to organize an independent Filipino Catholic Church which would still be under the authority of the Pope. About twenty-six clergy attended. It is important to realize that up to this point Aglipay and his supporters were hoping that the Pope would finally recognize their actions. They were not at this time separating from Rome — only from the Spanish clergy.

Political and military matters now took precedence over ecclesiastical matters. Aglipay was deeply committed to Philippine independence, so he took to the field as a general in the developing guerrilla warfare against the Americans. This fully occupied him until his surrender on May 25, 1901.

It was at this point that the second great leader of the emerging Independent Church entered the picture. This was Isabelo de los Reyes, Sr., a Filipino intellectual and writer who had been deported to Spain for his early pro-nationalist writings. Released from prison after the treaty of Paris, de los Reyes continued his writings. One of his books was *The Religion of the Katipunan,* in which he developed a liberal religion based on the ancient Filipino worship of the god Bathala. He translated the Bible into Ilocano. Hearing of the desire to form a national Church, he wrote an appeal to the Pope to recognize the Filipino leaders of the movement. He also wrote several articles supporting the war against the Americans.

After the surrender of Aglipay, de los Reyes decided to return to the Philippines. He arrived on October 15, 1901, and soon organized a labor union through which he hoped to propagate his views on social reform. The burning religious issue of those days was the "friar question" — Should the friars be expelled from the Philippines or not? De los Reyes and others were disappointed with Governor Taft's compromise solution. Taft had traveled to Rome and had persuaded the Pope to agree to the sale of the friar lands, providing that the friars themselves were not expelled. De los Reyes believed that they had to be expelled for the good of the country, and he became bitterly anti-Pope.

Moving ahead without the approval of Aglipay, de los Reyes announced the final break with Rome and the formation of the Independent Church on August 3, 1902. The surprised Aglipay disclaimed any connection with the move at first, but was soon convinced and accepted the title of Obispo Máximo — Supreme Bishop. On Sunday, October 26, 1902, Aglipay was formally inaugurated in Tondo, Manila, saying mass as Supreme Bishop before an open-air altar. The break was now clear and final, and the movement spread with great power. The fundamental grievance that led to the formation of this Church — the papal refusal to give Filipinos the leadership of their own Church — was only made worse by the apostolic constitution *Quare Mari Sinico* of Pope Leo XIII, promulgated on December 8, 1902. The Pope had again refused to elevate Filipinos to the bishopric, and he allowed regular priests to remain as parish priests.

Sometime during this period an important meeting was held. Bishop Aglipay and de los Reyes conferred with several Protestant leaders in Manila. The exact date of this meeting is an interesting historical puzzle, which research in original sources (including archival materials) has not yet finally resolved. Our two primary sources, Stuntz of the Methodists (1904a:489) and Rodgers of the Presbyterians (1940:20), were both at the meeting, but disagree about the date and the matters discussed — and even about exactly who was at the meeting. Most historians follow Stuntz, saying that the meeting was held in August, 1901. But since Stuntz is the one who mentions the presence of de los Reyes, his account must be in error, for de los Reyes was not yet in the country on that date. Rodgers speaks of the outdoor mass as having already occurred, therefore the date must have been in late 1902. The only other possibility would be that there were two meetings, but all sources agree that there was only one.

The results of this meeting were unsatisfactory for both groups. The Americans were put on the defensive by the evident Catholicism and nationalism of Aglipay. For his part, Aglipay found little encouragement from the Americans for his truly independent Philippine Church. Seen in its historical context, this was perhaps inevitable. The American missionaries and the Filipino leaders were wary of each other, although each looked to the other for support. If some mutual understanding could have been arrived at, the history of both groups would have been much different, but it would be unrealistic to have hoped that this could actually have been worked out at that time.

Meanwhile the movement spread. Ilocos Norte quickly became almost entirely Aglipayan. Masses of people from other provinces joined the movement, and soon it was claimed that the majority of Filipinos were members of the Independent Church. As this was a matter of allegiance, not of conversion, figures cannot actually be given for this period. For a time, probably the majority of the population (three to four million) were in sympathy with the Independents and were *potential* members. The religious practices of the new Church were the same as those of the Roman Church: masses were held, images were kept and the Marian cult practiced. The issue to most people was simply loyalty to Rome or loyalty to the Philippines.

On the premise that the Independent Church was now the Philippine Church, Aglipay claimed all the Church property and buildings in the Philippines. The property question thus became confused and of overriding importance. Taft tried to settle the question with his doctrine of "peaceful possession." That is, whichever group was in peaceful possession of a church building could use it. But the Roman Church could not accept this solution, and finally the case was brought before the Philippine Supreme Court and then to the United States Supreme Court. The decision was in favor of the Roman Catholic Church. Legally it could hardly have been otherwise, yet one thinks of the Church of England under Henry VIII. If the Philippines had been completely independent, the outcome might have been different.

This adverse property decision dealt the Independent Church a blow from which it has never recovered. What might have been a majority movement had become by 1960, after much attrition, a Church of 1,500,000 — a notable movement, but not the true national Church it had hoped to become.

As the Church grew, it quickly developed its own distinctive doctrinal position under the leadership of de los Reyes. What Melanchthon was to Luther, de los Reyes was to Aglipay — only to the detriment, not to the building up, of his theology. De los Reyes had been deeply influenced by liberal thought, so the Church rapidly became Unitarian and rationalistic in theology. Science was more of an authority than Scripture. Though moving with de los Reyes in matters of doctrine, Aglipay kept the Roman Catholic forms to which the people were accustomed. It is problematic as to how much of the Unitarianism and rationalism seeped down through the forms to the common people. Whittemore is undoubtedly right in criticizing the naïveté of the Unitarian leader Cornish, who thought that the Catholic ceremonies were mere forms which carried the Unitarian, liberal content, and that the movement had to be judged on the basis of the teaching, not the forms (Whittemore 1961:148-149, *compare* Cornish 1942:98-100). Whittemore, on his side, probably underestimated the doctrinal errors which were accepted in the Church.

Along with Roman Catholic forms, Aglipay was concerned about apostolic succession for his episcopal ordination. He approached both Bishop Brent of the Episcopal Church and the Old Catholic Church. Many Protestant leaders hoped that something could be worked out between Brent and Aglipay (see Briggs 1913:119). However, nationalistic feelings on both sides and doctrinal difficulties made this impossible. The Independent Church had to go through a generation of wandering before it could bring itself to return to the Creeds and join forces with the Episcopal Church.

Protestants have been criticized for ostracizing and underestimating the importance of this movement. Briggs, a Baptist, was an example of one who did see something of the significance of this Independent Church. He said:

I wish that every mission board in America would awake to the tremendous possibility that is open here today, but rapidly crystallizing into an impossibility and a forever lost opportunity, making this great movement Protestant and Christian at its fountain head. I believe that if St. Paul were prosecuting the evangelical mission enterprise in the Philippine Islands he would aim today for Aglipay and his counselors, as he headed away from Jerusalem and Judaism and Asia to Rome. . . .

Aglipay is a strong thinking man, trained in all the cunning casuistry of Rome and needs a stronger personality than his own to carry him from his sacerdotalism (Briggs 1904:225).

It seems unlikely that any American "St. Paul" could actually have communicated tellingly with the strongly nationalistic Aglipay.

How should we then evaluate the early history of this movement? It seems that it can be best understood as a Philippine indigenization of Roman Catholicism. There are certain parallels between the Philippine experience and what happened in England under Henry VIII. In both cases political motivations were strong — even overriding. The Church of England rose as an indigenous Catholic Church, so too the Philippine Independent Church. The differences, however, were important. First of all, England was completely independent. Henry VIII was the head of Church and State. In the Philippines the revolution had failed, and alien rule still prevailed. Then, theologically the Church of England had its Bishop Cranmer. Aglipay had de los Reyes. Social and historical factors are important, but what a Church believes and teaches is of final importance, for this is the work of God as well as men.

The first accurate membership statistics of the Independent Church are found in the 1918 census, which gives the number of community as 1,417,418. This date was long past the peak of the movement in 1904—1906. One evident weakness of the movement was its inability to sway more of the Filipino Roman Catholic clergy. Achutegui and Bernad claim that only about 50 out of a total of 825 Filipino priests joined the movement (1961:Vol. 1, 231-232).

SUMMARY

The beginning of Protestant missions in the Philippines was marked by great enthusiasm on the part of the missionaries and real responsiveness on the part of the people. Actual growth was determined primarily by how vigorously evangelism and church planting were carried out.

The fragmentary nature of Philippine society and the American character of the introduced Protestantism hindered the development of any large-scale people movement into the Protestant Churches. The possibility of small movements, however, was demonstrated by both the Methodist growth in Bulacan and the Baptist experience in Panay.

The early missionaries quickly grasped the basic realities of the Philippine social structure. The classes were never particularly receptive to Protestantism, so the early missionaries correctly decided to concentrate upon the barrio masses. Yet barrio evangelism does not seem to have been pressed as it should have been as the

Church developed. The missionaries too easily swung to an emphasis upon education.

There seems to have been a commendable minimum of competition and overlapping of efforts due to the splendid spirit of cooperation among the early missions. Yet even here concern for unity may have eclipsed efforts toward growth, especially after 1930 as the United Church was being formed.

But most important, the rise of the independent Churches, IEMELIF as well as Aglipayan, and Iglesia ni Cristo cried out for the indigenization of the Church. Missions have been too paternalistic and protective. Turning real authority over to Filipinos as quickly as possible was the crying need. If missionaries had continued to work on the extension of the Church and had left the young Church more in the hands of the Filipino leaders, both the slowdown in growth and the unhealthy Americanization of the Church which developed might have been avoided, or at least minimized.

CHAPTER 8

RECENT HISTORY AND MODERN PHILIPPINE SOCIETY

The Philippines presents a luminous case study of the influence of historical and social factors on church growth. The major divisions of Philippine history correspond so exactly with the introduction of new cultural influences and with the major movements of the history of the Christian Church in the Philippines that clear distinctions can be made and valid generalizations formulated. We have observed the entrance of Roman Catholic Christianity into late sixteenth century Philippine society under the conquest of Spain. We have seen the arrival of Protestant Christianity at the turn of the twentieth century with the American acquisition of the Philippines. Now we come to the contemporary scene of post-Independence Philippines with its developing nationalistic society. Here again we will lay the groundwork for the discussion of the growth of the Church by summarizing the major historical developments and describing the major features of the modern social structure.

INDEPENDENCE AND RECONSTRUCTION

On July 4, 1946, the dream of the Philippine nationalists, early and late, was fulfilled — but under circumstances that they could hardly have wished. Over two hundred thousand people gathered on the Luneta (a public park near the place where Rizal was shot) to watch the lowering of the American flag and the raising of the flag of the new Republic of the Philippines. Paul V. McNutt read the proclamation of Philippine Independence signed by President Truman. The newly elected President Roxas responded for the Philippines. Later that day General Douglas MacArthur said to Carlos Romulo, "Carlos, America buried imperialism here today" (Romulo 1955:5).

The tragedy of that day was that the man who had worked and fought so hard for its coming was not there to see the fruition of his labor. That man was Manuel L. Quezon. Throughout almost the entire period of American occupation, Quezon had been the articulate leader of the Philippine nationalist movement. When the Commonwealth government was formed in 1935 under the provisions of the Tydings-McDuffie Act of 1934, Quezon was elected the first President of the Philippines. It had been agreed that the Philippines would be granted its full independence on July 4, 1946. The threat of Japanese invasion which lay over the young Commonwealth became a reality on December 8, 1941. The heroic but hopeless defense of Bataan and Corregidor is well known. President Quezon was evacuated to Australia and then to the United States, there to await the liberation of his country. Tragically, tuberculosis took his life and he died on August 1, 1944.

On October 19, 1944, General MacArthur's troops landed on the island of Leyte, and the liberation of the Philippines began. Because of the fanatical resistance of the Japanese, the process of liberation wreaked great destruction, particularly in and around Manila. The once beautiful Spanish walled city (Intramuros) of Manila was completely destroyed. Loss of life was great. The production facilities of the country were destroyed. Yet the Americans were looked upon as liberators, and the granting of Philippine independence in 1946 was marked by a sincere spirit of amity between the two nations.

The economic prostration of the nation at the time of independence could not have been foreseen at the time when the date was set twelve years previous. For the fledgling Republic to survive, massive aid was needed. In response to the need, the United States Congress passed the Philippine Rehabilitation Act providing the payment of war damages, and the Philippine Trade Act extending the free trade arrangements for another eight years, to be followed by a period of gradually increasing tariffs. In these Acts we meet the same mixture of altruism and self-interest on the part of the United States which had marked its relations with the Philippines from

1898 to that time. In this case the Philippines had to amend its constitution to grant parity rights to American citizens and corporations in the exploitation of the country's natural resources. This "parity clause" has increasingly become a focus point for much anti-American feeling in recent years. Fortunately, many of the inequities of the 1946 Trade Act were removed in the 1955 Laurel-Langley Agreement.

The aid given by these acts helped meet the immediate threat, but did not solve the basic economic problems of the country. The *cacique* (landowner) controlled peasant economy was at the heart of the problem.

In 1946, this agrarian unrest gave rise to the greatest threat which the young republic has faced in its brief history — the Communist-inspired "Huk" rebellion. This movement has its roots in the troubled early 1930's, when the Socialist Party was formed in the Philippines. In 1938, the Socialists and the Communists joined forces and grew strong in the plains of Central Luzon, where the land problem was most severe. During the war this coalition formed a guerrilla force known as the Hukbo ng Bayan Laban sa Hapon (Army of the People against Japan). This was shortened to Hukbalahap and then to Huk. These guerrillas fought bravely against the Japanese, but refused to give up their arms after the war and thus became an armed menace to the new government. Taruc, the Huk Supremo, felt that the victory of Roxas "doomed the nation to a new puppethood and placed it under the shadow of fascism" (Taruc 1953:226). Roxas refused to seat Taruc and six other Huk-supported congressmen from Central Luzon. Now the smoldering dissatisfaction burst into armed conflict.

In April, 1948, as the rebellion was spreading, Roxas died suddenly and was succeeded by President Quirino. Quirino held out the olive branch to the dissidents, but after a brief respite the rebellion began again and spread. The scandal-rocked re-election of Quirino in 1949 did not help matters. The people began to lose confidence in their new government. The Philippine Constabulary and Army troops often proved more rapacious than the Huks. By 1950 the Huks were moving about at will through the islands. A reign of terror was instituted and symbolic acts of violence were perpetrated — such as the ambush and murder of Mrs. Quezon,

widow of the late President, and her party. In the face of this crisis
Quirino made a crucial appointment. In September, 1950, he
appointed the then little known Ramon Magsaysay to the post of
Secretary of National Defense.

Magsaysay – Turning the Corner

Magsaysay at the time of his appointment was a member of
Congress. He had not risen by power of family, but through personal
qualities of leadership. A man of great energy and purpose, he was
ideal for the sensitive position of Secretary of National Defense. His
greatest asset was his rapport with the common people. The
Philippines needed a charismatic leader – and they found him in
Magsaysay.

As Secretary of Defense he immediately plunged into a massive
reorganization of all the armed forces. Discipline was enforced and
morale lifted. Toward the Huks he employed a two-pronged
approach. In the light of his own wartime guerrilla experience, he
adopted new and effective field tactics. In this he was aided by the
newly formed Joint U.S. Military Advisory group. While pressing
forward the military campaign, he began to offer amnesty to Huks
who would surrender, with the added inducement of free land in
Mindanao. This dual approach began to gain results. Almost
immediately after Magsaysay took office a repentant Huk, urged on
by a cash reward, gave Magsaysay the information he needed to
capture the twelve top members of the Politburo in Manila along
with their complete plans for the takeover of the Philippine
government. The back of the Huk movement was broken.

It was no surprise that in 1953 Magsaysay was overwhelmingly
elected President. With great energy, but somewhat lacking in skill,
Magsaysay plunged into a program of social reform. Old-time
politicians were scandalized when Magsaysay opened Malacanang
Palace to all who wanted to bring him their troubles – "bare feet in
the Palace." True, this was not a very realistic way in which to deal
with the problem of State, yet Magsaysay achieved what was
desperately needed at that time. He restored the confidence of the
common people in the government, without which a democracy
cannot long endure. With the restoration of confidence, the
Communist threat was broken.

Nationalism and Economic Development

Magsaysay's career was tragically ended by a midnight air crash on March 17, 1957. By that time the initial enthusiasm for reform had begun to wane, and the older political realities began to reassert themselves. Vice-President Garcia succeeded to the Presidency and was re-elected in November, 1957. He sought to continue the program of his predecessor, but his administration lacked the spirit of radical reform of Magsaysay, and the old political bosses again made their influence felt. His Vice-President, Diosdado Macapagal, was of the opposition party and spent much of the four years of Garcia's term preparing for his own campaign in 1961.

Macapagal defeated Garcia in that election and slowly began to steer the Philippines into a more Asian orbit in keeping with the nationalistic spirit of the times. With Sukarno of Indonesia he worked, rather unsuccessfully, towards the formation of the Maphilindo (*Ma*laysia, *Phil*ippines and *Indo*nesia) alliance. Anti-American feelings were now more commonly expressed, and the Philippines began to shed its "American puppet" image in foreign affairs.

Internally, industrialization was progressing, but economic problems were becoming increasingly difficult and Macapagal could not seem to cope with them satisfactorily, nor to fulfill his campaign promises adequately. This set the stage for the election in 1965 of the present President, Ferdinand Marcos.

Through the various administrations certain political patterns have become evident. There is a greater centralization of governmental authority in the person of the President than in the United States. Party membership is largely based on personal loyalty to a leader and not on ideological issues. Regionalism is still quite strong; Garcia brought with him many fellow Boholanos, and Ilocanos are said to be much in evidence in Malacanang now, during the administration of Marcos. Once this is said, it must be quickly added that the Filipinos are quite successfully adapting the democratic forms to fit the political and social realities of their nation. They have created one of the few viable democracies in the Orient. Probably the most serious problem yet remaining is the still yawning gap between the upper classes and the great masses of the people. Economically the nation still has far to go, but the strides forward in recent years bide well for the future.

PRIMARY FORCES OF SOCIAL CHANGE AT WORK TODAY

To state that Philippine society is changing is not to repeat a trite statement but to point out a basic characteristic of Philippine life today. It is a society consciously on the move. In describing contemporary Philippine society the dimension of social change must be seen. Business and politics are awake to the changes occurring. The Church cannot afford to be less aware of them.

Many factors in Philippine society make it receptive to change. Prolonged exposure to both Spanish and American cultures has enabled extensive acculturation to occur. Modern means of communication, the presence of alien advocates of change (such as Peace Corps personnel and missionaries), returned travelers and repatriates — all have contributed to the presence of many new-felt needs and have shown the possibility of their fulfillment.

Within this climate of receptivity, there are several important forces at work for change. We will look at these separately.

Population Growth

The dramatic drop in the death rate caused by the introduction of modern medicine and hygiene, combined with the rural emphasis on large families, has given the Philippines one of the fastest growing populations of the world. Its present rate of growth is estimated at 3.5 per cent per annum — about 1,000,000 per year. The growth can be seen in the following table:

Year	Population
1600	500,000
1750	830,000
1800	1,561,251
1845	3,488,258
1903	7,635,426
1918	10,314,310
1939	16,000,303
1948	19,234,182
1960	27,087,686
1968	35,900,000 (estimated)

(Sources: Blair, Robertson:1903:Vol. 1, 86; Hunt *et al.*
1963:313; Population Reference Bureau 1968)

In 1900 the Philippines was definitely underpopulated. In 1968 some areas were facing seriously crowded conditions: the lowlands of Luzon, especially near Manila, and the Central Visayas. The large island of Mindanao can still be considered underpopulated.

Not only is the population growing, it is also increasingly mobile. Modern forms of transportation, including the airplane, have made a tremendous impact on the Philippines. Along with this mobility, internal migration is taking place. Two general patterns may be noted. People from the more densely populated areas of Luzon are migrating to other areas of Luzon. The surplus population of the Visayan area is moving to Mindanao. Underlying these general population movements is the great movement into the cities – particularly Manila.

The population is comparatively young, with 47 per cent of the population under 15 years of age. It is, however, becoming older as life expectancy increases.

Population growth is expected to continue at about the present rate of over 3 per cent per annum. Within two decades the Philippines will be one of the ten most populous nations of the world (McHale 1966:227), so this rapidly growing and increasingly mobile population will continue to be a force for change for many years to come.

Urbanization

Although the majority of the people still live in rural areas and in small towns, the cities of the Philippines are growing rapidly. All of the cities are sharing in this growth, but Manila stands out as the focus of this movement to the cities. In the 1960 census, the population of the Philippines was 27,087,686. About 8 per cent of this or 2,200,000 were within the metropolitan region of Manila.

In understanding urbanization in the Philippines, Ginsburg's concept of the Primate City is helpful. A Primate City is "a city with many times the population of the next largest city and a multiplicity of functions and attractions which give it dominance" (Ginsburg 1955:455). The importance of the Primate City in Southeast Asia is explained by Ginsburg as follows:

> A major characteristic of urbanization in Southeast Asia is the functional dominance, with two minor exceptions, of one great metropolis in each of the countries of the region. These cities have acted as the head-links between the West and the

indigenous societies. They are in a state of rapid social change, associated with the granting of political autonomy to the former colonial nations, with the accelerated rise of nationalism, and the increasing centralization of political functions in the national capitals (1955:455).

In 1960 about 5,600,000 or 21 per cent of the population was classified as urban. This is actually a lower percentage than the one given for 1948 (24.1 per cent) thus reversing the trend between 1939 and 1948 when urbanization was proceeding at twice the rate of the population growth. At first glance this might seem to contradict the claim of rapid urbanization. However, one problem is the definition of what is urban, another is that the total population itself increased by about 70 per cent. This means that many of the towns that are still classified as rural are growing so rapidly that they may soon become urban centers themselves. If this happens, McHale's prediction that by 1980 one half of the population will be urban could well become true (1966:228).

We will be describing the different aspects of urban society below. It is important here only to note that with the population growth, increasing urbanization is inevitable, and with increasing urbanization will come great economic and social changes. The Christian Church will be increasingly concerned with the urbanized communities. The reader should be reminded, however, that the rural population has been recently growing about as rapidly as the urban. As the Church plans for its future in the cities, it must also reach the barrios today.

Changing Economic Structure

With urbanization comes a shift from the agricultural economy to an industrial economy. In 1950, only 11 per cent of the total national income was from industry; by 1966 this had reached 19 per cent. This also means that the economy is becoming increasingly monetized, especially in urban areas. This disparity would seem to indicate that more and more people will be forced into the market and wage economy. We can then expect an increased monetization of the entire economy in the future. The economic aspirations have been raised by education, mass media and especially by exposure to American advertising techniques. McHale feels that this increasing monetization will lead to a more highly integrated national economy (1966:230).

Education

The impact of the educational system introduced by the United States into the Philippines can hardly be overestimated. This school system was effective in producing an educated, unified society with a working countrywide language — English. And as Wernstedt and Spencer have pointed out, "The American schoolteacher was the agent of cultural change reaching far beyond the language instruction thus provided" (1967:128-129).

McHale predicts that there will be an acceleration of the move from a semi-literate to a literate culture in the next several decades. The participation rates, for example, of primary school-age children will probably increase from 67 per cent to 95 per cent in the twenty years between 1960 and 1980 (McHale 1966:231). Education will increasingly become a major acculturating force in Philippine life.

Mass Communications

With the introduction of the transistor radio a new era began in mass communications in the Philippines. Lucena City (50,000 population), where this writer has been living, for example, has seen the building of three 5,000-watt radio stations within the last eight years. Previously there was none. It is predicted that

> by the 1980's it is likely that radio and television together will be theoretically capable of reaching over three-fourths of the Filipino population at any one point of time. . . . This will accelerate the shift from personality manipulation on the face-to-face level to symbol manipulation in the Philippines and the emergence of a "mass" culture (McHale 1966:230-231).

The Christian mission must be aware of these new factors in its planning for future propagation of the Gospel. Mass media techniques will become increasingly important.

Government

The introduction of secularized, representative government by the Americans set in motion many powerful forces for social change. The concept of directed social change is the rationale behind the numerous efforts of the government in community development. It is beyond the scope of this book to discuss this in any detail, but it must be pointed out that the government is quite active in this area. Much of the anthropological and sociological research done today in the Philippines is being carried out under government sponsorship. Thus the government itself is a powerful agent for social change.

PHILIPPINE SOCIETY TODAY

The Family

The overriding reality in Filipino social life is still the family. It is the most important element in Philippine social organization. Whether in politics, economic life or religion, the family has a central place. Philippine politics has been described by one author as an "anarchy of families" (quoted in Ravenholt 1962:130).

Structurally the family has changed little, except in the highly urbanized areas. The bilateral kinship system for the lowland population is shown in the Appendix. This diagram shows the structure as it actually is today. Its validity for the earlier period had to be substantiated from other sources. The main influence of acculturation on the kinship terminology system has been the dropping of some of the older Tagalog (or other dialect) terms and the use of Spanish terminology for some of the relationships (see diagram). In some areas English terms are beginning to be used; for example, *ongkel* (uncle) and *ante* (auntie) in Ilocano.

Overshadowing all other forces for change acting on the family today are those associated with urbanization. Mary Hollnsteiner has given a helpful threefold division of Philippine society, in terms that more clearly describe the changes which the impact of urbanization is bringing about. Those living in the urban centers, especially Manila, make up the first group. The second group comprises the communities on the urban fringe which are under the ever-expanding shadow of the cities. The third group consists of the more remote rural populations which are minimally influenced by the urban centers (Hollnsteiner 1963:3-4). Rather than to regard these three types of communities as distinctly separate, it would be more accurate to visualize them as representing segments on a continuum. Reflected in this analysis is Redfield's folk-peasant-urban continuum, although the divisions do not exactly correspond. Even the remote lowland farmer would probably be classified as "peasant," reserving the "folk" category for the tribal mountain people.

The family in the remote rural area has naturally undergone the least change. The rural Filipino finds his security within the family group. The relationships within this group are clearly defined and reinforced by patterns of respect which are ingrained from childhood. His relations with non-kinsmen are rather delicate. His kinship web defines for him his world to which he is deeply obligated and from which he can expect support. The picture is very little changed from the earlier periods in Philippine history.

In contrast, those living in the urban centers, particularly Manila, are finding that the traditional family structure is breaking down rapidly. Much research is being conducted in this area to see what is actually happening. It is clear that today the urban society is in a state of flux, and many families are experiencing great tension as the traditional norms come in conflict with the social realities of the present. The urban population is characterized by an increased mobility. Greater production and concentration of wealth have improved the standard of living, thus increasing the economic pressures on the families as their level of aspiration is raised. Young people are changing jobs and moving away from home more often. Young couples are eloping more frequently. And in contrast with the strong pattern of generational respect in the traditional culture, many families are experiencing a "generational conflict" (Ravenholt 1962:133).

One of my Tagalog informants who was born and raised in Manila confirms this great change in the family in Manila in contrast to the family in the provincial areas. He spoke of not knowing who many of his cousins are, and of the lack of respect for the parents common in many Manila families. This does not mean, however, that the traditional family structure is dead in Manila. Family ties still mean a great deal — especially when applying for a job!

In his study of urban families in Malate, Manila, Eslao found a rather surprising development in urban family life. He found that the extended family household was quite common, especially of the nuclear-lateral type (nuclear family plus siblings of one of the spouses) and of the nuclear-joint type (two related nuclear families) (1966:206). This was in contrast to the culturally preferred type of single nuclear family households. Eslao probably correctly attributed this to the difficulty of obtaining decent low-cost housing. It should also be pointed out that the traditional family structure was much more congenial to this development than the American-type family structure would have been. The single nuclear family household was preferred, but not obligatory.

The associational type relationship, rather than strict kinship relationships, has come into prominence in urban Philippine society. There is still a strong aversion to the "loner." The club, gang, or informal grouping is now important. *Barkada* is the Tagalog term for this concept. The ties of loyalty and mutual aid formerly associated only with family are now being transferred to the *barkada*.

The middle or urban fringe communities show many of the characteristics of the urban society, but to a lesser degree. Family ties are stronger, but there is the growing importance of the associational group. Hollnsteiner outlines the four basic social relationships in this type of transitional community:

1. *Kinship* — including consanguinity and affinity. This is bilateral in extension with the nuclear family of primary importance.

2. *Compadrazgo* — The ritual kinship or *compadre* system [described on page 90]. This effectively broadens the kinship web rather extensively.

3. *Reciprocity* — the donor-debtor relationship based on *utang-na-loob* (debt of gratitude) that permeates modern Filipino society. This includes landowner-tenant relationships.

4. *Associational* — This is an alliance system which is held together by ties of kinship, *compadrazgo* or reciprocal obligation to which others may join themselves — often motivated by self-interest (1963:64ff.).

Within these transitional communities the traditional kinship structure remains quite strong. The elements of generational respect are retained and many of the traditional marriage patterns are followed, only with a movement toward simpler and more economical arrangements.

The Barrio

We have already seen how the barrio developed from the older *barangay* communities as the *barangay* became a territorial, not a kinship, unit. The barrio maintains its importance today as the majority of Filipinos still live in these rural communities. With the growth of the total population the number of towns has increased only a little, while the number of barrios has increased greatly. In

1903 there were about 1,000 towns and 13,000 barrios; in 1960 there were 1,300 towns and nearly 26,000 barrios. Wernstedt and Spencer point out that with the growth in population some barrios have grown quite large, but the more common has been "the hiving off, or splintering off, tendency of the Filipino, which has resulted in the founding of new sitios and new villages." They also indicate that most barrios now contain one primary village (administrative center) and numerous *sitios* (hamlets) (1967:165).

In discussing urbanization a distinction has been made between communities which were remote from the urban centers and those which were on the "urban fringe." In the same way, it is helpful in discussing the social structure of barrios to distinguish between the more remote barrios and those that are town-oriented; that is, that are closely connected with a somewhat urbanized town or city. All barrios are not the same and one should be careful about broadly generalizing concerning them.

As we come to describe class distinction, the problem of the choice of criteria arises. Many investigators, such as Pal and Lynch, have decided that the only really measurable criteria are the economic ones. On this basis they have found the existence of only two basic social classes in rural Philippines. The common characteristic of the upper class, according to Pal, is economic surplus. By contrast, the basic characteristic of the lower class would be an economic deficit in terms of the felt needs of the people. The landowner, the *cacique,* is still the typical upper class person in the rural areas. The share tenants and day laborers are representative of the lower class. In his research in Negros Oriental, Pal discovered that in the barrios the lower class outnumbered the upper class about twelve to one (1966:39). He also found that the upper class tended to move out of the barrio into the *población.* In contrast to Pal's two-class structure, Ethel Nurge found a three-class structure with an emerging middle class in the barrio of Leyte which she was investigating. Her criteria were also economic. However, she made a distinction between those who have a "ceiling" in their earnings − a low ceiling, at that − and those who had a "floor" below which they did not receive. The latter were government clerks, teachers and *pensionados.* These constituted her "emerging middle class" (Nurge 1965:42).

It is probable that both analyses are valid, but that Pal's is more applicable to the remote rural barrio, while Nurge's three-class structure would more adequately describe the society of a town-oriented barrio. It is significant in this connection that Pal notes that in Negros Oriental, non-farm job opportunities are negligible, which is certainly not true in the town-oriented barrios of many areas of Luzon. On the other hand, it is also true that the elite are so far above Nurge's so-called middle class that this class is really not "middle" but upper-lower. The basic two-class structure then holds with the emerging "middle" class modifying the social structure in the town-oriented barrio.

Leadership in the barrio is personal. There is no "council of elders." The barrio councils which have been recently organized by law have not yet become an integral part of barrio society. Disputes are usually settled by a mediator, or by a recognized leader, or even by a *cacique*. A person who is able to weave a web of obligation about him can become a leader even if he is not wealthy. The barrio *lider* (leader) has become an important political figure in modern Philippine life. He is often elected *teniente del barrio* (barrio lieutenant) and will hold office as long as his political "boss" in town is in office.

In planting churches in the barrios these patterns of leadership should be traced out carefully. Because of the basically fragmentary nature of Philippine society as a whole, cliques and factions are common within a barrio, and these can be important in setting the patterns according to which a movement can grow in a given barrio. Key converts can mean great growth in the barrio, but blocked-off web movements can easily occur, also.

Towns and Cities

We will discuss the town and city together, partly because of the difficulty of classification in the Philippines and also because they actually form a continuum. Manila, being in a class by itself, will be discussed separately.

First, the meaning of the term *chartered city* in the Philippines must be explained. This term has a strictly political meaning and does not necessarily reflect a social reality. A chartered city is a town or city which has been granted a charter removing it from the control of the provincial government and placing it directly under presidential administration. Thus it does not necessarily denote an urbanized area. Manila was the first chartered city, Baguio the second. By 1963 there were 63. Lieban explains:

Most chartered cities of the Philippines outside Manila are "fractional cities," containing large amounts of farmland, sometimes forests, within their boundaries, and urbanized to a very limited extent in terms of their total area. Cebu is an exception (1967:15).

It should be added that ordinarily the granting of a city charter does recognize the leadership of the city in a particular area, and that generally the chartered cities are more urbanized than the towns surrounding them. One working definition of a city is that "it is a town that enjoys a measure of leadership among towns" (Dickinson 1964:21). If this definition is accepted, most of the chartered cities would qualify as cities.

The modern towns have mainly developed from the old Spanish *pueblos*. The town is the seat of the political administration of the surrounding area. Since the higher classes have tended to congregate in the towns, professional services such as medicine and dental care are normally available only in town. The town market is the commercial center for the region, and the town church is the religious center. There is usually good jeepney service between the town and its various barrios which are accessible by road, and the towns themselves are usually joined together by provincial bus service. The economic status of the towns varies widely. Community development seems to be more rapid in the chartered cities, for they are usually in favored areas and more easily claim the personal attention of the President.

The social structure of the town and the small city is still marked by the same basic two-class division that characterized them in earlier times. Only now the picture is more complex because of increased social mobility. The elite are no longer simply the landed gentry. The professional and successful entrepreneurial groups now must be included. Here again the continuum is important. The more rural-oriented the town, the sharper is the distinction between the upper and lower class, and the greater is the disparity in numbers. The more urbanized the town, the more numerous are the upper classes, and there is definitely an emerging middle class. This rising middle class consists mainly of salaried government employees, teachers and successful small-business people, as well as the lower rung of the professionals. These middle class people still live on a much lower economic level than the elite, so they still must be sharply distinguished from them. The lower class wage earners, laborers, and domestic servants still constitute the bulk of the population.

What is the basic power structure of the modern town? In her work *The Dynamics of Power in a Philippine Municipality* (1963), Mary Hollnsteiner points out that there are two types of political elites — the traditional (*cacique* type) and the newer professional-entrepreneurial types. These elite groups have lower-status allies who function as links between them and the masses. These are the *liders* who keep the political patronage system operating. They are therefore very influential people. This same pattern is seen in a modified way in the town church. The local priest has his patronizing elite group and also his group of *liders* through whom the masses can be mobilized.

This is still very much a face-to-face society. Leadership is personal, and communication follows definite channels determined by the systems of personal alliances.

These basic leadership patterns should be further studied by Protestant leaders. We need to find out what this means for a truly indigenous church organization.

Manila — The Metropolis

We have already classified Manila — in the sense of the greater Manila area — as the Primate City of the Philippines. In 1960 it was about ten times the size of its nearest rival, Cebu City. Ginsburg points out that Manila, like most great cities of Southeast Asia, was historically a foreign creation, and in a sense alien to the indigenous culture (1955:458). As such, it served as the "head-link" between Western civilization and the native society. Since Independence, Ginsburg would term Manila a "link capital"; that is, it is the link of the newly independent nation to the outside world. Contributing to this function is its character as a port city. In this role it is experiencing a revitalization of the indigenous Philippine culture, illustrated by the recent change of traffic signs from English to Tagalog, as well as the contradictory increase of Western, particularly American, cultural influences. As a result of these factors Manila, in common with the other great cities of Southeast Asia, is increasingly marked by cultural pluralism. This is also seen in the various ethnic groups active in the city. Chinatown in Manila stands in sharp contrast to the American-dominated Malate area, for example.

To describe the social structure of such a heterogeneous society is very difficult, for one must specify of which "Manila" he is speaking. Some areas of greater Manila are quite cosmopolitan (Makati, for example) and contain people of many racial backgrounds. Others are more exclusively Filipino. One schematization of Philippine social classes (found in Eggan 1955:438b) shows the various social groupings ranging from the rich landowners and professionals down to the newly arrived *provincianos*. The dimension of complexity is introduced by the presence of the various ethnic groups (such as American and Chinese) and the *mestizos* (mixtures) from Asian to European and American.

Striking through the complexity, however, is the economic barrier which divides Manila into the classes and the masses − the "haves" and the "have nots." This basic two-class division is still a reality in Manila, though a diminishing one. A few years ago the sociologists were speaking of a "nascent middle class," but now it would be more proper to speak of a "growing middle class."

Much about the social structure of the less cosmopolitan areas of Manila resembles that of the urban-fringe towns which we have mentioned. The leadership patterns in these areas reflect the same type of alliance systems. In Manila, kinship counts for less, but alliance webs built around lines of mutual obligation are common.

In visualizing Manila society we must keep in mind the basic fact which is illustrated by the diamond-shaped diagram that we have used before. That is, that the "haves" represent only a very small minority of the population, while the masses of the people remain very poor. This is still the cause of many deep-rooted social problems which have helped produce a severe crime problem in the Manila area.

The tendency to fragmentation, which we have mentioned as one of the basic facts of Philippine society, is graphically seen in the numerous districts and sub-districts of Manila. A Manilan thinks of himself as a resident of Paco, Sampaloc or Tondo, rather than just of Manila. The Roman Catholic Church has been able to adapt to this diversity more easily than the Protestants through their system of parish churches. Protestants have tended to be strong in one district and weak in others.

As the Church faces the City, it must be aware of its dynamic patterns of growth — the movement of its population along the highway, and the suburbanization of industry which has begun. A great building boom is progressing both in the suburbs and in the downtown area, where many obsolescent buildings are being replaced by new structures. All of these factors point to the growing industrialization and the increasing urbanization of Manila society. The task of effective evangelism in this burgeoning metropolis is one of the great challenges facing the Christian Church in the Philippines today.

CHAPTER 9

THE CHURCH IN A CHANGING SOCIETY

One of the important lessons of history concerning the Roman Catholic Church is its viability. One reason for this viability is its international character — what this Church prefers to call its "catholicity." This internationality is of a special kind, however, for it is under the authority of the Roman papacy. Nevertheless, it was this internationality that saved the Roman Catholic Church in the Philippines.

The aftermath of the Philippine Revolution and the American acquisition of the islands left the Roman Church demoralized and in a state of disarray. This was shown by the early expansion of the Independent Church. Archbishop Nozaleda and several other Spanish bishops were removed and were replaced by American bishops. Under Archbishop Harty, these men fought for the retention of their buildings, and this was assured by the court decision of 1906. Although they lost the friar lands, they received the healthy sum of $7,000,000 for them.

Of more than one thousand friars in the islands in 1898, only 246 remained in 1903 — although more were soon to arrive. In 1907 the Provincial Council was convened to reorganize and revitalize the Church. One of the Council's first moves was to emphasize the training of Filipino clergy. Several Filipinos were raised to the bishopric at this time.

Since the early American period, two rather contradictory trends have developed in the Roman Catholic Church in the Philippines.

One is the commendable emphasis on the nationalization of the clergy. In 1934 a Filipino archbishop was appointed. In 1960 Cardinal Santos was elevated. By 1958 the Jesuit order in the Philippines had a Filipino majority. On the other hand, the regular priests, the friars, have streamed back into the country — this time mainly from non-Spanish orders.

The 1965 Roman Catholic statistics showed one priest for 5,638 Roman Catholics. The total number of priests was 4,175, of which 1,935 were diocesan (secular) priests and mostly Filipino, and 2,240 were "religious" (regular) and mostly foreign (Gowing 1967:243). Today many of the religious have been assigned to schools in Manila and other urban areas, so this effectively reduces the ratio of priest to member even further, and indicates how undershepherded many of the rural areas are, even by Roman Catholic standards. A great effort is being made on the part of the hierarchy to encourage vocations among the student population. Devout Roman Catholic families are likewise put under great obligation to give one of their sons to the priesthood if possible.

Latourette (1962:364) says that Catholic Action (a movement that promotes participation of the laity in the apostolate) was introduced in 1939, but has had little success. Since he wrote this, the movement has taken on new life and has become increasingly active in community affairs. In 1966 Catholic Action members conducted a successful community crusade to rid Lucena City, and later other cities, of night clubs which had become fronts for prostitution. Student Catholic Action groups also have been growing in strength, sometimes at the expense of such interdenominational organizations as the YMCA.

One of the most effective movements in present-day Roman Catholicism in the Philippines aimed at mobilizing laymen is the *cursillo*. The *cursillo* (little course) refers to the program of highly organized religious retreats for men and, recently, for women. In this program, laymen are invited to a retreat center for a weekend of intensified instruction in dogma, Scripture and liturgy, combined with a highly structured devotional discipline. At the end of the retreat they are asked to take a special Catholic Action vow in which they promise to maintain faithful family prayers and pledge loyalty to the Church and abstinence from certain vices. I have also been informed that they promise not to read any Protestant or "sectarian" literature. The appeal of prestige in the movement is strong, as the leaders of the community are the first ones to be requested to attend these retreats. They in turn seek to recruit others — especially their associates or employees. Everyone who takes the vow wears the gold dagger-cross which is the symbol of the movement.

The Roman Catholics operate an extensive school system throughout the Philippines. They are opposed to the public school system in principle, but pragmatically try to infiltrate it through the textbooks and special religious instruction. In 1965 there was a total of 1442 Catholic schools with a combined enrollment of 604,037 students (Achutegui and Bernad 1966:397). In addition, they have sought to pass laws making the teaching of religion compulsory in the public schools. Their system of colleges and universities is notable. Santo Tomas University, founded in 1611, is the oldest university in the Philippines. The Jesuit Ateneo de Manila is academically one of the finest schools in the country.

The winds of change coming out of the Second Vatican Council have blown across the ecclesiastical scene of the Philippines. A spirit of renewal is noticeable in many areas of church life. Liturgical renewal has been stressed as masses are being said in the local languages and in English. Hymns are being sung and a new Misa ng Bayan (Mass of the People) has been introduced, based on the concept of the Church as the people of God. The new emphasis upon the use of the Bible is seen in the recent excellent Tagalog translation of the entire Bible and apocrypha by Abriol. Many new ecumenical contacts are being made between the Roman Catholic and Protestant clergy, even to the extent of invitations to Protestant ministers to preach in Roman Catholic chapels. A new day in which the Roman Catholic Church will sincerely accept the fact of religious pluralism in the Philippines may be dawning.

THE DECLINE OF THE PHILIPPINE INDEPENDENT CHURCH

The Philippine Independent Church has never regained its early initiative and growth. As the population of the Philippines has increased from about 10,000,000 in 1918 to about 33,500,000 in 1967, the membership of the Philippine Independent Church has remained at about 1,500,000. The decline is seen when this is translated into percentages. In 1918 this Church accounted for about 15 per cent of the population; in 1967 it represented less than 5 per cent. Evidence of this decline is visible in the deteriorating local church buildings and the grave lack of priests in the Church.

After the death of Aglipay in 1940, and after the Second World War, the Philippine Independent Church began its painful journey back to Catholic orthodoxy. A split occurred as Fonacier and de los Reyes, Jr., struggled for control of the Church. A long series of court cases ensued, until in 1955 the Philippine Supreme Court declared Bishop de los Reyes, Jr., the legitimate Supreme Bishop of the Independent Church.

Bishop de los Reyes became convinced that the future of the Independent Church lay with the American Episcopal Church. Through the years of court litigation, de los Reyes, Jr., was negotiating with the Episcopalians for recognition of the Philippine Church. He indicated the Aglipayans' readiness to accept the Catholic creeds, including the article concerning the Trinity. The Church also agreed to rewrite their Declaration of Faith, Articles of Religion and Constitution.

In 1947 the Episcopalian St. Andrew's Seminary in Manila agreed to train priests for the Independent Church, and the two Churches drew closer together. Also in 1947 the Aglipayans voted to petition the American Episcopal Church for the historic episcopate. In November 1947, this request was approved by the House of Bishops of the Protestant Episcopal Church; and on April 7, 1948, in an impressive service in the Pro-Cathedral Church of St. Luke in Manila, three Filipino bishops, including Monsignor Isabelo de los Reyes, Jr., were consecrated in the Anglican line by the Rt. Rev. Norman S. Binsted of the Philippine Episcopal Church.

The climax of these moves came at the 60th General Convention of the Protestant Episcopal Church, held in Detroit in September 1961. At the convention a concordant was approved which granted full communion to the Independent Church. This was a concordant of intercommunion, not union. Yet, practically, it meant that the Episcopal Church was now free to give the Philippine Independent Church the help, including financial aid, that she so desperately needed.

Although renewal is now seen at the level of ministerial training, it is difficult yet to observe any noticeable revitalization of the movement at the local level, but it is to be hoped that this will come as the new priests filter out into the parishes. A great task of evangelism awaits them among their own people.

Bishop de los Reyes, Jr., himself has been warmly received by many of the larger Protestant Churches. He was the first President of the National Council of Churches in the Philippines — an outgrowth of the former Federation of Christian Churches. The Independent Church is the largest member of this new body.

THE GROWTH OF THE IGLESIA NI CRISTO

As the Aglipayans have now moved more into the orbit of the American-oriented Churches, the torch of religious nationalism and anti-Trinitarianism has passed to another young and vigorously growing Church — the Iglesia ni Cristo. This "Church of Christ," which is the meaning of the name, is sometimes called the Iglesia ni Cristo, 1914, to distinguish it from the Church of Christ movement which originated at a much earlier date in the United States, and to draw attention to what they consider the very significant year in which it was founded by Felix Manalo.

Felix Manalo, the founder of this Church, began his religious pilgrimage just after the turn of the century. In 1904 he was converted to Protestantism under the Methodists and began to study for the ministry under them. Then he transferred to the Presbyterian Ellinwood Bible Training School. He was then attracted to the teachings of the Disciples of Christ (which his Iglesia ni Cristo biographer constantly confuses with the Christian and Missionary Alliance!). Convinced of their position on baptism, he became one of their early evangelists. In about 1912, he was converted to Seventh-Day Adventism and began to work for them. However, he soon became disillusioned and in 1914 struck out on his own. On July 27, 1914, after an initial period of teaching his new doctrines and gaining a few converts, he incorporated the new Iglesia ni Cristo. His biographer indicates that in these early days Manalo drew many of his converts from the Disciples, and refers to the early beginning of the practice of engaging in religious debates regarding the eating of blood, worship of images and baptism (Garcia 1964:181-182).

In 1919 Manalo came to the United States to study one year at the Pacific School of Religion. He returned to find his infant Church rent by division. He re-established his own leadership and the Church began to expand. Apparently growth in these prewar years was slow, but it did begin to spread into some of the provinces, especially those close to Manila.

After Independence, the movement spread rapidly over the country. In the years 1946 to 1956, churches were begun in nearly every province. Statistics are notoriously difficult to get from this very exclusive Church, and exaggeration is common. Villanueva, one of their apologists, writes:

> The Iglesia ni Cristo has rapidly spread to almost all of the provinces, cities, towns, barrios, and fields, and today is reaching millions of members, not only in the Philippines, but likewise in Okinawa, Hawaii, Guam, the United States, Wake Island, and other places (1964:21, translated from the original Tagalog).

It must have come as a shocking disappointment to them to see the 1960 census figure of only 270,000 members, though even this figure means that it is much larger than any of the Protestant Churches. Even allowing for some error in the figure and allowing for extremely rapid growth in the last few years, it would seem unlikely that the total membership today exceeds 600,000. There is even reason to believe that their great rate of growth during the 1950's and early 1960's has now decreased since the death of Felix Manalo in 1963. Nevertheless, their postwar growth has been phenomenal and their wealth and power can be seen in their large churches (which they prefer to call chapels), of which they are so proud. In many cities the Iglesia ni Cristo Chapel is more imposing than the Roman Catholic cathedral. The 50th anniversary issue of their magazine *Pasugo* had eighteen full pages of photographs of local churches (*Pasugo* 1964:53-70).

What are some of the factors which account for the great growth of this Church?

1. A dogmatic and exclusive message, which is clearly presented. They teach that on the basis of Romans 16:16, the only true Church disappeared in early history, but was restored in the Philippines in fulfillment of the prophecy in Isaiah 43:5-6. Manalo, its leader, fulfilled the prophecy of Revelation 7:2-3, predicting the rise of an Angel of the East. They claim that the teachings of the true Church are to be found only in the Bible *as interpreted by the Sugo* (the Sent-One). These teachings include salvation by joining the true Church (Iglesia ni Cristo), baptism by immersion and abstention

from eating blood — the eating of which is the sin against the Holy Spirit. (It should be noted that *dinuguan,* a dish made from cooked blood, is a Philippine delicacy.) They rigorously deny the Trinity, teaching that Jesus Christ was a man who, although the Saviour, had no pre-existent state.

2. Effective use of public debate. Their debaters are intensively trained to defend their own position and demolish opposing viewpoints.

3. Reactionary anti-Catholicism. This feeds on the underlying dissatisfaction of many with the Roman Church.

4. A completely centralized and autocratic organization. All message outlines originate from the Manila headquarters. No private interpretation is allowed.

5. Effective mobilization of workers to cover the various districts and barrios of the towns.

6. Direct appeal to the masses, combined with the ostentatious display of wealth by their leaders for prestige. The leaders are quite conscious of the social class structure and use it to their advantage.

7. Highly disciplined membership. Attendance at Sunday and Thursday meetings is required. Specified amounts must be given in the offerings regularly. Every member is required to vote according to the precise instructions given him by the leaders. Excommunication is frequent. (This is a source of statistical error, for many are baptized who do not stay with them, yet continue to be counted.)

8. Economic aid and strong emphasis on patronizing their own members in business. Members will seek to employ other Iglesia members whenever possible.

9. A strongly nationalistic emphasis. This is one of the most powerful appeals. The Tagalog language is the official language of the Church, although in other areas the local language may be used. The members are taught that the Philippines is God's chosen nation of the last days.

10. The Church's absolute indigenous nature.

If Aglipayanism can be regarded as an attempt at indigenization of Roman Catholicism, the Iglesia ni Cristo may be an attempt at indigenization of Protestantism. If this is a valid analogy, it demonstrates the need for a more effective indigenization of Protestant Christianity and for the removal of the American image that is all too visible in much of Philippine Protestantism today.

THE CHALLENGE TO EVANGELICAL CHURCH GROWTH

The Older Churches

As the Philippines began its career as a newly independent nation, the most important development among the older Protestant Churches was the formation of the United Church of Christ in the Philippines. The movement toward actual union began in 1929, when the Presbyterian, United Brethren and Congregational Churches organized themselves as the "United Evangelical Church of the Philippines." In 1948 this Church joined forces with the Philippine Methodist Church (a break-off from the larger Methodist Church of the Philippines) and the Evangelical Church in the Philippines to become the United Church of Christ in the Philippines (UCCP). Later the Disciples of Christ joined the United Church. The UCCP, uniting as it does a great number of Protestants over much of the Philippines, has exerted a decisive influence in postwar Philippine Protestantism. Its growth graph indicates that, except for a slowdown in the mid-50's, it continued to grow until 1963, when it plateaued for three years before resuming its growth again in 1967. Some of this growth may be "merger growth"; that is, growth due to the joining of other Churches, such as the Disciples of Christ, which joined the UCCP in two stages (the Tagalog branch having only recently joined).

The Methodist Church, the largest Protestant Church before the UCCP merger, has actually lost members, if the graph is to be believed. There are serious problems in Methodist statistics for this period, however, which may have masked actual growth. The large drop in 1954 was the result of the dropping of the "inactive member" category in the statistical reports. That significant growth has indeed occurred would be indicated by the fact that in 1948 only 356 local congregations were reported, while in 1968 there were 684.

These two large Churches are now facing a serious problem in providing an adequate ministry for their churches, especially in the rural areas. The hopeful sign is that they are aware of the problem and are experimenting with some new patterns of ministry.

The Philippine Baptist Convention continued its pattern of little growth well into the postwar period until about 1954. Since then the growth has swung upward to show almost a 100 per cent decadal

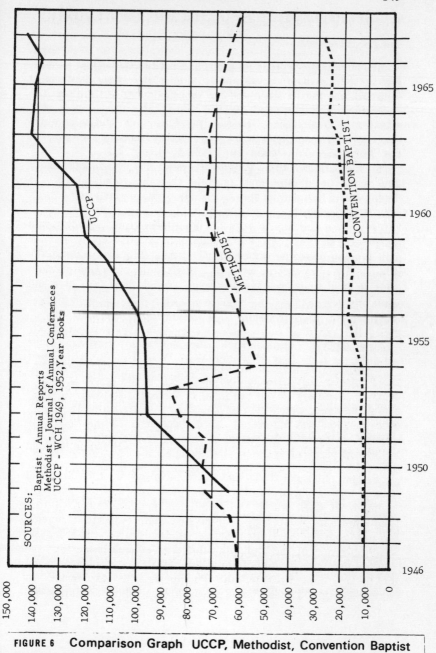

FIGURE 6   Comparison Graph   UCCP, Methodist, Convention Baptist

growth. This increased rate of growth significantly coincided with a marked resurgence of evangelistic activity, especially in the province of Negros Occidental. Large budget allocations for evangelism, combined with energetic Filipino and American leadership, enabled the Convention Baptists to double the number of their churches in Negros between 1953 and 1958. Evangelistic activity also radiated from Central Philippine University during this period under the direction of its president, Dr. Almus O. Larson. Dr. McGavran notes the evangelistic activity of the gospel teams from the university in his Philippine survey (McGavran 1958b:128).

In evaluating church growth statistics in post-Independence Philippines, it is important to note that the population of the Philippines is growing at the rate of about 30 per cent per decade. Thus the membership of a Church should at least show this rate of growth if it is to keep up with the population growth. A lower rate of growth, such as that of the Methodists, would indicate that the children and young people of the members are not being kept in the Church. Here lies the challenge of growth to the older Churches not only to hold their own, but to make fresh advances for Christ and His Church.

The Newer Churches

One important element that makes the current Protestant scene so different from that of the pre-World War II period is the great influx of new missions into the Philippines since World War II. Related to this has been the growth of other missions and Churches, which although not strictly post-War, did not make their major impact until after the War. These new missions and Churches fall broadly into three categories — the Pentecostal Churches, the interdenominational "faith" missions and the newer denominational missions.

Several interrelated factors were involved in this historical development. Liberal theology, combined with a strong emphasis upon social work within the traditional denominations, led to a multiplication of strongly conservative and evangelical mission organizations in the United States, especially after the War. The disorganization of the Philippine Churches as an aftermath of the War resulted in a vacuum of evangelistic effort that challenged many of these groups to enter the Philippines. The experiences of concerned United States' servicemen in the Philippines during and immediately after Liberation resulted in the formation of at least one mission — the Far Eastern Gospel Crusade. Then, too, some missions which had been formed to reach specifically the "unreached" tribal areas of the world — the New Tribes Mission, for example — were challenged by the many tribes of the Philippines which had been largely neglected in the prewar period.

Then came the closing of China to foreign missionary work. By 1951 China had fallen to the Communists and this had an almost immediate effect on missions in the Philippines. Many of the missions that had been working in China began investigating the possibility of working with the "overseas Chinese" in Southeast Asia. As these missions entered these countries, and especially the Philippines, they became aware of the needs of other groups as well and began to broaden their ministry. The China Inland Mission became the Overseas Missionary Fellowship (OMF) and began to work in Manila with the Chinese at Grace Christian High School in 1951. In that year also the OMF sent their first missionaries to the tribal peoples of Mindoro, and in 1956 began their evangelistic and church-planting work in Bauan, Batangas, among the lowland Filipinos (Dirige 1966:32-34).

The Assemblies of God is representative of the Pentecostal Churches which, although they entered the Philippines previous to the War, did not achieve great growth until the postwar period.

The first Assemblies of God missionaries to the Philippines were Mr. and Mrs. Benjamin H. Caudle, who arrived in Manila in September 1926 (Esperanza 1965:17-18). Due to health problems they were unable to continue. The actual beginning of the work was through Filipinos who had come to the United States to study or work, and while in the United States became convinced believers in the Pentecostal doctrine, trained in a Pentecostal Bible Institute and finally returned to their own country to preach the Gospel and spread the Pentecostal message among their own people. Cris Garsuelo, returning home to the province of Antique in about 1930, was the first of these Filipino missionaries. The movement spread, and at the close of 1939 American missionaries, Mr. and Mrs. Leland Johnson, came to work with the young Church. War came, the Americans were interned, but the Church continued to grow.

By 1949, 1822 members were reported. In 1952 there were 2,193. Then the Assemblies of God entered a new phase of rapid growth as the large Bethel Temple in Manila was begun under the

ministry of Lester Sumrall. This church, which became the largest
Protestant church in Manila, had its beginning in a series of
large-scale evangelistic and healing meetings in 1952 and 1953. The
turning point came with the healing of a young 17-year-old girl,
Clarita Villanueva, who was then an inmate of the Manila City Jail.
The newspapers and radio were reporting her experiences of
allegedly being beaten by demons which only she could see. Sumrall,
hearing of this, offered to go and pray for her. After fasting for two
days, he prayed for the girl, commanding the demons to depart. The
girl was delivered, and the press gave the event great coverage. In
gratitude the Manila City Council passed a special ordinance to give
Bethel Temple its needed building permit free of charge (Esperanza
1965:48, 49). Soon the building was completed, and because of the
slogan, which has almost become the Philippine Assembly of God's
trademark, the church is known to many Filipinos simply as the
"Christ is the Answer" church.

By 1958 the Assemblies of God reported a membership of 12,022
– an increase of almost 500 per cent in five years! The reported
membership in 1968 of 26,285 shows a healthy decadal growth rate
of about 118 per cent, but it does represent a slowdown in growth.
What happens in the next few years will be crucial in determining
the future of Pentecostalism in the Philippines.

Besides the interdenominational missions that have entered the
Philippines and the Pentecostal Churches that have begun a new
phase of growth, there have been several new denominational
missions which have arrived since the War, some because of the
closing of China. These include the Southern Baptists, the Lu-
theran Church – Missouri Synod, the Evangelical Free Church, the
Baptist General Conference, the Conservative Baptists and others.
Since I am a member of the last named group, the Conservative
Baptists, I will describe the work of this mission and its young
Church as somewhat representative of this group of missions and
Churches.

Beginning in 1948, Conservative Baptist missionaries came to the
Philippines to work with other Churches and missions. One
missionary, Miss Beulah Heaton, taught at the interdenominational
Far Eastern Bible Institute and Seminary (hereafter referred to as
FEBIAS), which had been begun by the Far Eastern Gospel Crusade
while another couple came to work with the Far East Broadcasting
Company. A short time later the William Simons family was forced

out of China by the Communists, and coming to Manila found a place of service at Grace Christian High School, an independent school for the Chinese. The Conservative Baptist Mission was not engaged in any type of church-planting activity in the Philippines at that time. Mr. Simons was soon convinced that there was still a need for this type of mission work in the islands. In 1952 the Home Board of the CBFMS passed an official action to begin church-planting work of its own in the Philippines.

In 1954 Simons carefully surveyed the church-planting needs of the various areas of the Philippines in an extensive trip throughout the islands. He came to the conclusion that one of the most needy areas at that time was the southern Tagalog region of Luzon. Under the 1901 comity agreements this had been part of the Presbyterian area. Now, however, he felt that the United Church of Christ (into which the former Presbyterian Church was incorporated) in that area was in a state of deep decline. Further, it seemed that the area was being passed over by other evangelical missions which were reaching out to the more remote areas. The area that was chosen in which to begin work lies in the eastern part of southwestern Luzon.

Several Baptist laymen in Manila who had received some training in an evening Bible institute were anxious to see a new evangelistic outreach begun in the shore towns of eastern Laguna province. The Communist-led Huk guerrillas had been quite active in the area, but this threat had recently been brought under control so that missionaries could now enter. A very small staff of missionaries (one couple and a single lady) working with the laymen from Manila and assisted by students from FEBIAS began a regular evangelistic outreach into several of these towns. Within three years a group of five small churches had been started around the lake. The evangelistic and pastoral work was carried on by several older pastors formerly associated with another Baptist mission, and the laymen.

In 1959 an important decision was made to begin a church in the Manila area. This added a completely new urban dimension to the work. The same year work was begun in Quezon province, which lay along the southern border of Laguna province.

The Conservative Baptist Association of the Philippines was organized in 1961, an outgrowth of an earlier association known as the Fellowship of Baptist Churches in Southern Luzon. In 1967 this Association entered into a cooperative agreement with the Mission in which they have equal representation on the joint committees which direct the overall work of evangelism, Christian education and literature.

By 1968 the young Church had grown to a total of thirteen organized churches, four unorganized groups called chapels, and nine preaching points with a total baptized membership of 1,010.

Characteristic of many young Churches begun by postwar missions is a high missionary-to-communicant ratio. Note the following table of missionary strength and communicant membership for the conservative Baptists:

Year	Missionaries	Communicant Members
1955	5	30 (est.)
1956	9	100 (est.)
1957	16	150 (est.)
1958	21	190 (est.)
1959	20	227
1960	22	300 (est.)
1961	23	432
1962	23	472
1963	23	591
1964	23	630
1965	23	636
1966	27	762
1967	26	845
1968	26	1010

(Source: Annual Reports, CBM; estimates by author)

In evaluating these statistics several factors need to be taken into consideration. First, not all of these missionaries have been engaged in direct evangelistic and church-planting activities. Some, for example, were on the staff of a school for the education of missionaries' children. Some had to leave the field for medical reasons, or to serve on other fields. Then, too, many of the missionaries were involved in intensive language study for various lengths of time. Nevertheless, it cannot be denied that a high missionary-to-communicant ratio exists. Many of the new Churches and missions show this same characteristic. This high ratio may be defensible in the beginning stages of the work, but as time goes on, if great growth does not occur, there is a grave danger that missionary-dominated, encapsulated Churches will emerge, which can multiply only with great difficulty.

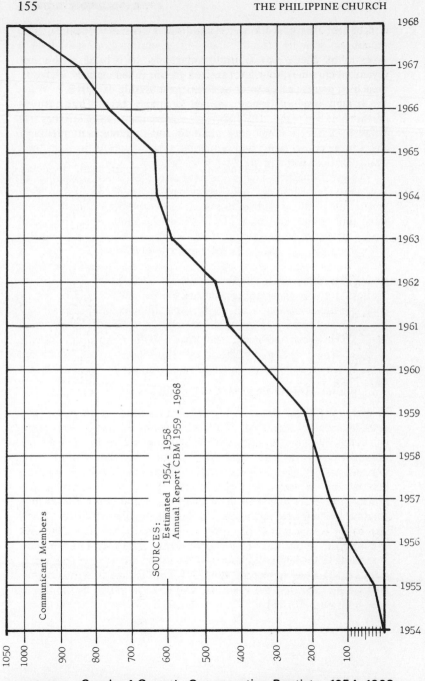

FIGURE 7   **Graph of Growth Conservative Baptists   1954-1968**

The fact that new Churches such as the Conservative Baptists are growing in what is actually a second generation Protestant field is both an advantage and a disadvantage. A new Church's nominal-Christian membership is at a minimum, for it does not yet have to deal with its second generation. Yet there is also the sense in which the ground has already been burned once and much of the newness of the appeal is gone. The future growth of these new Churches will be very instructive. Will they only fill in the unreached corners of the country, or will they contribute significantly to the total evangelization of the nation?

The great question facing the new Churches today is whether or not they can develop new patterns of growth in this second generation field. To do this, missionaries and Filipino Church leaders must understand the social structure of the Philippines today and devise strategies to work effectively within it. A few are doing this with some success. Programs of family evangelism have begun, for example. But much more needs to be done. Instead of using unadapted evangelistic methods which have been successful in Western cultures, new approaches are needed. We should be asking such questions as, How can we win the Filipino family for Christ? How can we evangelize the great socially complex, urban center of Manila? How can we reach the barrio, both remote and not so remote? These and many other questions need to be asked and answers found before we can effectively multiply churches in the Philippines today.

CHAPTER 10

HOW THE CHURCH CAN GROW IN THE PHILIPPINES

In this historical-sociological investigation we have traced the development of Philippine lowland society from its sixteenth century Malayan baranganic form to the modern, Americanized Hispanic-Malayan society that it is today. We have seen that it has been, and now is, a society in which the Church can grow. Because the Church does not grow in a vacuum, but in a context, the way the Church has grown in each period has been profoundly influenced by the historical and social realities of that period. It is but reasonable to assume that this also will be true in the future. The historical forces at work will be part of this context, as will the prevailing social structure and the patterns of leadership and communication. Religious and spiritual factors will also be part of the total context — a most important part. If all external factors are favorable to growth, but obedience to Christ is lacking, the growth, if any, which takes place may be of little value. Yet, on the other hand, if the Church, fully dedicated though it may be, blunders ahead in blind disregard for the social and historical realities of the situation, it will be doomed to little or unhealthy growth instead of the sound growth it could have achieved.

IMPERATIVES FOR GROWTH

Restricting our view to the Protestant Churches, what then are some of the imperatives with which our findings confront us?

1. *The American captivity of the Church must end.* The Spanish period in the Philippines has much to say to the modern Church concerning the need for indigenization of the Church. To make the Church indigenous to the native culture, Spain endeavored to re-shape the early Malayan society. To some extent she succeeded. She succeeded because of the length of time during which she had complete political control of the islands. Yet, in the end, the Roman Church was still completely governed by the Spanish bishopric. We have seen how the power of nationalism exploded in the early rise of the Philippine Independent Church.

When the United States took possession of the Philippines, she, too, sought to reshape Philippine society somewhat in her own image. She wanted the Philippines at least to have democratic institutions like her own, and to have an educational system that would tend to Americanize the culture thoroughly as time went on. Did the early Protestant missions tend to presuppose this progressive Americanization of the Philippine culture? Their enthusiasm for the educational program of the United States and their lack of sympathy for the nationalistic aspirations of the Filipinos may indicate that they did. It appears, too, that the early enthusiasm for learning the languages and dialects of the people dimmed as English made headway in the schools.

But all of this is in the past. The Philippines is now a free and independent nation. The forces of cultural nationalism have been gaining more and more influence, especially since the presidency of Macapagal. The experiences of the late nineteenth and early twentieth centuries warn the Church not to disregard the voice of the nationalists as perhaps representing only a small and insignificant segment of the population.

Sober Filipino voices are being heard in the Church pressing the need for increasing Filipinization of the Protestant Church in the Philippines. Perla Dirige, in the concluding chapter of her thesis, questions whether there is a real national Church in the Philippines (1966:69-83). She points to the fact that in 1965 the Methodist Church had to appeal to the United States Church for help when it became deadlocked over the election of a bishop. She mentions that most Manila churches have an American missionary to help the national pastor. American books are used in the churches, and in fact almost everything in many evangelical churches is Western —

including the order of service. Larson describes worship services in a remote barrio chapel in which "regular as clockwork they sing the first verse, the second, and the last verse of the hymns" (1963:174).

A Lutheran missionary once told me that the most Americanized group of Filipinos with which he had come in contact were the evangelical Christians. Personal observation would tend to substantiate this statement. I once witnessed a harvest festival service in a UCCP church held on Thanksgiving day — an American holiday that is sometimes noted in the Philippines but not actually observed by the masses of the people. The season of the year was wrong for the harvest theme, and the message focused on the experiences of the American Puritans. Gadiel Isidro, a Filipino, speaking generally of the Churches in the Far East says, "the national churches there have tended to be Americanized to an unhealthy degree" (1966:297). This is surely true of the Church in the Philippines.

What are some concrete steps that should be taken to stimulate the growth of a more healthy indigenous Church? In asking this question we are not suggesting that all American influences be removed from the Philippine Church. That would be simple reaction and actually not true to the cultural realities of present-day Philippines, which is truly Americanized to some extent. What, then, should be done?

1. The large churches in Manila should be turned over as quickly as possible to responsible Filipino leadership. This step should not be taken in fear. In the Conservative Baptist Capitol City Baptist Church, for example, this step was taken in April 1967 as four American families left places of leadership in the church. The church found the first four months rather difficult, but a year later it reported a 22 per cent increase in attendance. The quality of English may or may not suffer, but the Church's calling is not to the preservation of the English language.

2. Filipino music and liturgical patterns should be developed. The Iglesia ni Cristo has pointed the way in this matter. All of their anthems are sung in Tagalog in contrast to the average Protestant church where, even if the rest of the service is in the area language, the anthem will be sung in English because printed choral music is readily available in that language.

3. The use of the vernacular Bible should be encouraged. This is especially important for pastors, most of whom were trained in English. They are most familiar with the English Bible and often are

not at home in the Bible in their own mother tongue. Related to this would be the suggestion that in the Bible schools and seminaries at least one course in Bible be given in the language of the area. Now all courses are taught in English. It might also be helpful if some of the homiletic courses were conducted in the vernacular.

4. Methods need to be devised that would not tie the multiplication of churches to the presence of the foreign missionary. Although the Pentecostal Churches are pointing the way in this matter, even among them the American tends to be used as a prestige symbol and a rallying point for the new churches. New patterns of partnership between American missionaries and Philippine national missionaries need to be developed.

5. Finally, because of past American emphasis, the Philippine Protestant Churches need to be self-consciously Philippine and not American. This also means that the missionary must adapt himself to the local culture, including language, in a way that he previously has not. In other words, he needs to adopt a host culture orientation. What this means is summarized by Pal:

> Any attempt to introduce changes in the life of a people should, above all other considerations, be for their welfare. If it is for their welfare, then the program to introduce changes should endeavor not to disorganize the host culture. . . . The approach may be called the *host culture orientation* (1956:7).

2. *The family must be reached and won.* This is the second imperative, for in every period the basic unit in Philippine society has been the family. In spite of increasing urbanization, it still is. But simply recognizing this basic sociological fact is not enough. A program must be devised. One program that is meeting with some success in both rural and urban situations is that of "Family Evangelism" as conducted by some missionaries and pastors in Conservative Baptist churches. Family Evangelism is the plan of evangelism which aims to bring whole family units to Christ through a program of home Bible studies.

Any program of mission that is adopted should meet the following criteria:

1. It must be culturally oriented. That is, it must work along with, not against, the dominant traits of a culture as much as possible (see Luzbetak 1963:180).

2. It must be biblical. It must be in harmony with the basic themes of evangelism found in the Word of God.

3. It must be workable. The available resources of the mission or Church must be taken into account.

4. It must communicate the Gospel. It must be such that God blesses it to the salvation of men's souls.

Let us use these criteria to evaluate the program of Family Evangelism.

1. Is it culturally oriented?

We have already seen in some detail the structure of the Philippine family and its significance in Philippine society. Let us now summarize these findings.

The Filipino family is the basic unit of Philippine society. There is the *elementary family* composed of father, mother and children. The *extended bilateral* includes all relatives of both the father and mother. This extended family can be made even more "extended" through the *compadre* system or ritual co-parenthood.

The roles of the father and mother are remarkably balanced in the Philippine family. The oppressed state of women, so typical of many oriental societies, is not present in Philippine life. In the matter of authority the father is the "authority figure," but not to such an extent that the society could be called patriarchal. The pattern of authority is definitely generational, based on age rather than sex. The sibling group is very important in Philippine life. The older siblings are accorded respect by the younger and in turn have certain definite responsibilities in matters of care and discipline. Often a grandparent will be in the household, and there is a very close relationship between grandparent and grandchild.

The family is the effective center of Philippine social life. Indeed, it is the most important element in Philippine social organization. The religious life of the family seems to center almost more in the family than in the church. Several observations support this statement. For example, whenever a big family event is occurring in the parish church, e.g., a wedding or baptism, even the anticlerical members of the family will attend. There are the ever-present family shrines in Philippine homes, and many wealthy families have their own private chapels. Filipinos will frequently go against canon law in asking non-Catholics to be sponsors at baptisms and weddings if they desire that some particular person be a *compadre*.

What does all of this mean for the missionary or national pastor seeking to preach the Gospel in the Philippine setting? It surely means that to be in any way effective, evangelism must take place in the context of this family structure. The first advantage then in the term "family evangelism" is that it focuses attention immediately on the family. This is no small gain in itself. To see the focus of our work correctly is to cross the major hurdle immediately, and the work can move ahead in harmony with this major cultural theme in Philippine life, and not against it.

The home Bible study method — that is, the holding of evangelistic Bible study classes in different homes — is a natural instrument to use in implementing this program. Being in the home means that the nuclear family along with the other members of the household will hear the teaching of the Gospel. Although individuals in the home will find it very difficult to make a decision alone, if there is a decision of acceptance it is usually a family decision. It has been our experience that usually the husband will make the first positive move toward acceptance, but the decision of the wife is crucial in deciding whether or not it will be a family decision.

Once the decision has been made, it is then a very natural development to follow out the bilateral lines of kinship. This will usually produce an abundance of contacts. Focusing upon the family in evangelism is a big step toward making it culturally oriented.

2. Is it biblical?

Our second criterion, from a theological viewpoint, should be first. Here we must examine the biblical data concerning evangelism to make sure we are working in harmony with the revealed principles.

In turning to the New Testament we note that there is an emphasis upon individual decision in following Christ. In Jesus' dealings with his disciples this is especially clear. The words of Christ that "He who loves father or mother more than me is not worthy of me" clearly show that following Christ is a profoundly personal act (see Matt. 10:34-39). But does this mean that the individual must act without any relation to others, in a vacuum, so to speak? It is plain that it did not work that way in the first century Church. Simon was brought to Christ by his brothers. In this regard the most important datum of Scripture that must be faced is the group of references to household conversions in the book of Acts. These instances are the households of Cornelius (11:14), Lydia (16:15), the Philippian jailor (16:31ff.) and Crispus (18:8). Referring to these passages Kast says:

> ... I must comment further on the problem of those peoples whose religious, social and economic systems are so tightly interwoven that one system cannot be changed without directly and immediately affecting the other system. This was true in the time of Paul when belief was often the simultaneous act of a whole family. The impression is that Jesus and Paul got through to the key members of families and the rest followed suit. This is quite consistent with our general picture of the oriental household whose head is ascribed almost absolute authority (1963:177).

It is a scriptural fact, then, that families, as families, believed and moved into the Christian faith together, and that the quality of their faith was not in any way questioned by the New Testament writers. Therefore, the emphasis upon winning families for Christ has clear scriptural support and thus meets the second criterion.

3. Is it workable?

Family Evangelism is really more of an emphasis than a particular method of work. Surely there are several workable means of presenting Christ to entire families and appealing for group decisions. One way is to witness to the head of the family and challenge him (or her) to decide with his entire family (e.g., the Philippian jailor). Another is to hold a special meeting at a home at which all of the extended family is gathered together (e.g., the story of Cornelius). We have found in our own experience that an organized program of home Bible studies is particularly effective. In this program the missionary and national pastor and workers have a definite schedule of home Bible studies in the homes of interested families. These studies are quite evangelistic in nature, and an effort is made to include as many members of the family as possible. The pattern of decision expected is the family pattern. There are materials which have been developed to use in these Bible studies. We have found it to be a practical method which can be used by many people. It is workable.

4. Does it communicate the Gospel?

Any human program must be evaluated in terms of the results

(McGavran 1959:144). In the last eight years we have observed this program in action in several towns and cities of the Philippines. Churches have been planted and built up through this method. But to help the reader visualize how this can actually develop in a particular situation, let us trace the way in which a particular family came to the Lord in the Lucena Baptist Church. The key to this family was the father, Mr. B. His brother and sister-in-law preceded him in accepting the Gospel, but it was not until his two older unmarried daughters, who were visiting their uncle and aunt, were converted and then returned home, that the missionary was put in contact with the father. A Bible study was started in the home, and within a month the basic decision was made by the father. Quickly the members of the household followed suit. It was not long before the married daughter and her husband were converted. Then the process jumped to another extended family through a *compadre* relationship of the son-in-law and the harvest continued. The Lucena Church was quite small at the time and this process, which took somewhat more than a year, doubled the membership of the church. Does it produce results? It certainly does, although not always this dramatically.

Scripture and experience teach that it is never easy to follow Christ, but let us not add unnecessary burdens to the process of conversion. To work with the culture of a people whenever possible is but the part of wisdom; to work against the culture is to make impossible the planting of a truly indigenous church.

3. *Present responsiveness must be met by growth.* This third imperative addresses itself to the Christian Church in the Philippines today because Filipinos are responding to the Gospel of Christ. This responsiveness is seen in almost every area of the Philippines, but not to the same degree. One of the tasks remaining for further research is to map out clearly the areas of greatest responsiveness. We will focus first on the responsiveness in the barrio, then in the town, and finally in the city, especially Manila.

a. In the barrio. Approximately three-quarters of the Filipinos still live in barrios, but the majority of the churches are in the towns. Historically, Protestant missions have found the barrios very receptive to their message, as we have seen. Even today, as churches analyze how they are growing, they are surprised many times to note that their growth is taking place through conversions in the barrio, even though the church building is located in the *población* (town proper). In the survey made by Dr. McGavran for the UCCP in 1957, he found that the typical UCCP church was what he described as the *"población* partly" type. That is, while the church and some members were residing in the *población,* many members were clustered in various barrios surrounding the town (1958b:14-15).

In the light of the masses of people still in the barrios, and their continued responsiveness, a definite strategy needs to be devised to reach the barrios for Christ. In planning for church growth in the barrios the fragmentary nature of Philippine society needs to be taken into account.

Pal found in his investigation of a barrio in Leyte that "each *sitio* within the barrio was an in-group in itself" (1956:73). Then, especially as the barrio school was developed, the larger barrio itself became a homogeneous group, as indicated by their common religious beliefs, endogamous marriage patterns and low mobility (1956:83). Each *sitio,* and to some extent each barrio, is therefore a true community which can be approached as a unit. Pal found especially important the role of the community leaders – particularly that of the "kinsman spokesman," whose primary function was to serve as intermediary for establishing the *compadre* relationships between his kin and others in the community (1956:129). The role of the community leaders cannot be overestimated, for the group as a unit cannot make any commitment without the approval of the leaders. The leaders thus become the "gate-keepers" of the group (Pal 1956:203).

Protestant missions have tended to emphasize the individual and the one-by-one approach in evangelism to the extent that often to become an evangelical Christian has meant that one must leave his social group. In some instances this is probably all that could be done. However, the most rapid and the most healthy growth occurs when people can move into the Christian faith within their own social group in a movement based upon multi-individual and interdependent decisions – in other words, in a "people movement." In view of the fragmentary nature of Philippine society, large-scale people movements are unlikely, but smaller family web-type movements should be expected and encouraged.

From this perspective it is clear that the *sitio,* and, if possible, the barrio should be approached as a unit. In beginning the work of evangelism, the community leaders, the "gate-keepers," should be first contacted and, if possible, their sympathy won. In community discussions the kinship spokesmen for the different extended families may be involved and should be followed up. The role of the key convert in web evangelism is extremely important. It is not unreasonable to expect whole *sitios* to declare for evangelical Christianity. It apparently happened in the early days of Protestant missions in the Philippines. Public meetings in the *sitios* and barrios, combined with systematic home Bible studies, would be a means for the harvest of family units in rapid succession if the barrio is responsive.

Looking at the task from a larger perspective, it would seem unlikely that all barrios of a town would be equally responsive at a given time. Some means of probing the barrios should be developed, possibly through the distribution of literature. The barrios which show the greatest response should be entered first. Many times members of the town church may be key "bridges" to responsive barrios.

If the evangelization of the barrios of the Philippines is to be pressed, leadership training for these barrio groups and churches must be developed. At first, this can be done by home Bible studies and correspondence courses, but later something more structured will be needed. One suggestion is the development of a system of extension theological education in the area language for the natural leaders of the churches. This probably would best be done cooperatively, by the various missions and churches in the same area. The program could be patterned somewhat after the Extension Seminary of the Presbyterian Church in Guatemala (Winter 1967).

The possibility of the extensive development of barrio churches might be questioned on the basis that this goes against the culturally accepted pattern of barrio people coming into town to attend church. If, however, growth was large enough in the barrio to see the birth of a church, there is no reason to think that the people would not like to have a church of their own led by their own folk, in their own barrio. Because of the relationship of the barrio to the town, however, it may be that the barrio churches should be related to the town church in such a way that the town church would become the mother church of the barrio churches. This seems to be the pattern of the Iglesia ni Cristo, which has many barrio groups, but which has built many imposing town church buildings with which the barrio people can identify.

The challenge for barrio evangelism has been well stated by Dr. McGavran:

> Recapturing great church growth in the Philippines depends to a large extent on winning barrio people and multiplying sound churches in barrios. Barrio people can be won. This is the universal testimony from all the islands. But a system which successfully organizes converts into rural churches which support themselves and reproduce vigorously is largely lacking (1958b:70).

To develop such a system is one of the great tasks still facing the Philippine Church today.

b. In the town (población). Not all of the towns of the Philippines have yet been reached for Christ, and many towns which have been reached have only a weak evangelical witness. Great growth is yet needed in the town. How can this be accomplished?

First, a survey should be made to see the extent of evangelical coverage in the towns of all the islands. There seems to be a tendency to overlap evangelistic efforts in some areas, while in others, usually more remote, towns go unreached for decades. A determined effort should be made to reach these unreached towns.

The outreach into towns with existing churches needs to be expanded. Unhealthy forms of religious competition need to be avoided, but a "dog in the manger" type of comity should not be allowed to deter the entrance of new churches into towns which show great need. This is a delicate matter, but religious and denominational pluralism is an increasing reality in the Philippines, and may actually not be uncongenial to the fragmentary nature of Philippine society.

In evangelizing towns we must concentrate on the family webs. In addition, the existence of distinct districts within the town must be noted. In many instances the social structure and leadership patterns within these districts are very similar to those of a barrio and should be dealt with in the same way. District evangelistic campaigns can be a very important means of growth for a town church.

The concept of "neighborhood churches" does not find ready acceptance in the Philippines. Whether or not churches of the same denomination can be multiplied within the same town is a matter which needs further investigation. It is, however, unlikely that one church can adequately minister to the population of a larger town. Churches must be multiplied.

Attention should be drawn briefly to the great responsiveness observable in the towns which are growing because of migration from other areas. Uprooted people often prove exceptionally open to the Gospel. Strategy for church growth should focus on these growing towns, especially in Mindanao.

c. In the city – Manila. Although the emphasis of this investigation has been on the rural lowland Philippines, enough has been said concerning Manila to indicate some of the guidelines which an effective approach to church growth in that great city should take. The recent rapid growth of several urban congregations gives some indication of the responsiveness. The Capitol City Baptist Church was begun in 1959 as a group of people meeting in homes to study the Bible. Its building was dedicated in 1965 and the church now has an average Sunday morning attendance of 220.

The first matter that needs to be taken into consideration in planning for church growth in Manila is that, taken as a whole, it is definitely not homogeneous, but it does contain a multitude of smaller homogeneous units. It is geographically divided into many districts, and each of these is divided further into subdistricts. Here again a survey is needed to find out how these various districts and subdistricts are being served by the existing churches. Are there large pockets of people outside the sphere of influence of any church? One suspects there are many. Are the various language groups, such as Ilocanos, Ilongos and Cebuanos associated with their own people in such a way that they can be treated as homogeneous units? What about the recently emerging middle class group? Are they being followed as they move into different areas of town – especially into the suburban areas?

The need for research in Manila is great. We need to find out among which groups, for example, the Iglesia ni Cristo is most rapidly growing. Their list of local churches is instructive and gives an indication of their penetration into the city. Their local churches in Manila proper are in Tayuman, Paco, Solis, Sampaloc, Quiapo, Barrio Obrero, Concha, Washington, San Nicolas Syquia, Pandacan, Punta, Sta. Ana, Dagupan, Balut and Barrio Magsaysay (*Pasugo,* July 1964:119), with a new large church just erected in Tondo. Few Protestant Churches have such coverage.

As in the case of the barrio, evangelistic probes should be directed into these different districts by different means and aimed at different levels of society, for not every social level will be equally responsive. The settlements of new arrivals to the city should be entered, using the language of the group, if it is homogeneous. Fruitful probes should be followed up by a program of evangelism, possibly home Bible studies.

As churches are formed in Manila, the high cost of land and buildings will become a problem. Mission and church resources may be used to break through this barrier at least initially. Then home churches could be emphasized by tying them into an existing church with a building as a mother church.

Many Manila churches have found that their lay leaders are very eager to enter lay leadership training programs. This desire should be capitalized upon by embarking on an expanded evening Bible school program — possibly again using the extension education approach. The training of the urban Filipino pastor is a matter which will increasingly concern the missions and Churches in Manila.

These are but a few preliminary suggestions, but growth *must* take place in Manila if the evangelical Churches are to grow and remain strong in the face of increasing urbanization.

At the conclusion of this survey of the growth of the Christian Church in the Philippines, we are deeply challenged by the responsibility which lies upon the Filipino Churches and their assisting missions to reach their expanding population for Christ in this particular period of opportunity. We are also deeply impressed with the need of the Church to be truly Filipino while remaining truly Christian and missionary. May the Church of Jesus Christ become increasingly effective in reaching the individuals, families, *sitios,* barrios, towns and cities of the Philippines for Christ and His Church.

APPENDIX:

TAGALOG KINSHIP TERMINOLOGY

The accompanying diagram shows the present-day kinship terms used among the Tagalog people. The informants were from Batangas province. The diagram follows the standard form used in sociological studies to portray the terms of reference; that is, the terms which are used by a person (*Ego*) to refer to his different relatives. *Ego* is at the center of the diagram, the older generations are above him, and the younger below him. A triangle represents a male; a circle, a female.

In some cases the Spanish (Sp) terms are more frequently used, but the older Tagalog terms are still remembered. The kinship terminology illustrates the bilateral character of the structure. It is predominantly what Murdock calls the "Eskimo" type; e.g., cousins are referred to by a different term than siblings. There is, however, some mixture of the "Hawaiian" system, especially in the use of the same term for the grandparents as for their brothers and sisters. The Tagalog terminology for uncle and aunt shows strong similarity to that of the parents, so this also may be a residual Hawaiian feature.

An analysis has been made of the kinship terminology of the Ilongo people (a major Visayan group). It was found to be of the same type — predominantly Eskimo with some mixture of Hawaiian (Gonzales 1965:24). This is not at all surprising since bilateral family structure is characteristic of the Malayo-Polynesian people in general, and particularly those of Southeast Asia (Murdock 1949:230-231; 1960).

171

FIGURE 8

TAGALOG KINSHIP TERMS

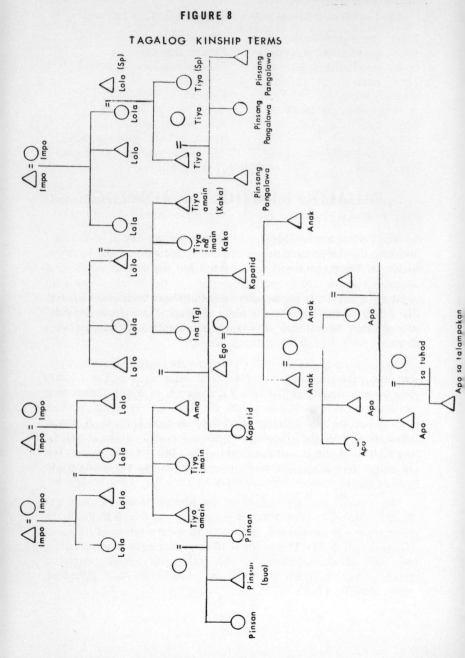

The English equivalents to the Tagalog terms are as follows:

Impo great-grandfather
Lolo grandfather, great-uncle
Lola grandmother, great-aunt
Tiyo uncle
Amain uncle
(not commonly used)
Tiya aunt
Imain aunt
(not commonly used)
Ama father

Ina mother
Pinsan cousin
Pinsang pangalawa second cousin
Kapatid sibling
Anak son or daughter
Apo grandchild
Apo sa tuhod great-grandchild
Apo sa talampakan great-great-grandchild

The terminology of address for older brothers and sisters referred to in the text is sometimes further refined as follows:

Siyaho eldest brother
Sangko 2nd eldest brother
Kuya 3rd eldest brother

Ditse eldest sister
Sanse 2nd eldest sister
Ate 3rd eldest sister

Significantly these terms can be shown to have been derived from the Amoy dialect of the Chinese, although the informants felt strongly that these terms were Tagalog not Chinese. Compare the above list with the following Amoy words:

hia^n-*ko* eldest brother
ji-ko 2nd eldest brother
sa^n-*ko* 3rd eldest brother

a-che eldest sister
ji-che 2nd eldest sister
sa^n-*che* 3rd eldest sister

It is beyond the scope of this study to investigate further the influence of Chinese culture on Philippine family structure, but it may well be that this particular feature of respect for difference of age within one generation was introduced into the Tagalog culture by the Chinese.

BIBLIOGRAPHY

ABUEVA, Jose V.
>   1959 *Focus on the Barrio.* Manila, Institute of Public Administration, University of the Philippines.

ACHUTEGUI, Pedro S. and BERNAD, Miguel A.
>   1961 *Religious Revolution in the Philippines,* Vol. 1. Manila, Ateneo de Manila.
>   1966 *Religious Revolution in the Philippines,* Vol. 2. Manila; Ateneo de Manila.

AGONCILLO, T. A.
>   1956 *The Revolt of the Masses.* Quezon City, Philippines, University of the Philippines.

ALIP, Eufronio M.
>   1947 *Political and Cultural History of the Philippines.* Manila, Alip and Brion Publications, Inc., Vols. 1 and 2.

AMERICAN BAPTIST CONVENTION
>   1966-67 *Year Book.*

AMERICAN BAPTIST FOREIGN MISSION SOCIETY
>   1911 to 1940 *Annual Reports.*
>   1941 to 1965 *Along Kingdom Highways* (Annual Reports).

AMERICAN BAPTIST MISSIONARY UNION
>   1902 *Annual Report.*
>   1906 to 1916 *Annual Reports.*

ANDERSON, Gerald H.
>   1964 "Missionary Readings on the Philippines: A Guide," *Occasional Bulletin.* July-August.

BALAGTAS, Fransisco
>   1947 *Florante at Laura.* Manila, Philippine Book Company.

THE BAPTIST MISSIONARY MAGAZINE
>   1900 May
>   1900 July
>   1901 September
>   1903 July
>   1904 July
>   1905 July

175

BARNETT, H. G.
    1953 *Innovation: The Basis of Cultural Change.* New York, McGraw-
         Hill Book Company.
BARROWS, David P.
    1925 *History of the Philippines.* New York, World Book.
BEACH, Harlan P. and FAHS, Charles H., eds.
    1925 *World Missionary Atlas.* New York, Institute of Social and
         Religious Research.
BEACH, Harlan P. and ST. JOHN, Burton, eds.
    1916 *World Statistics of Christian Missions.* New York, Committee of
         Reference and Council of the Foreign Missions Conference of
         North America.
BEYER, H. Otley
    1921 "The Philippines Before Magellan," *Asia*, 21:861-892, 924-970.
BEYER, H. Otley and DE VEYRA, Jaime
    1947 *Philippine Saga, A Pictorial History of the Archipelago Since
         Time Began.* Manila, The Evening News.
BIBAY, Bienvenido Aquino
    1965 "Membership and Statistical Records of the Methodist Church in
         the Philippines: 1913-1963." An unpublished B.D. thesis, Union
         Theological Seminary, Palapala, Dasmarinas, Cavite.
BINGLE, E. J. and GRUBB, Kenneth G., eds.
    1952 *World Christian Handbook – 1952.* London, World Dominion
         Press.
    1957 *World Christian Handbook – 1957.* London, World Dominion
         Press.
BLAIR, E. H. and ROBERTSON, J. A.
    1903-1909 *The Philippine Islands 1493-1898,* 55 vols. Cleveland, Ohio,
         Arthur H. Clark Company.
BLOCH, Marc
    1964 *The Historian's Craft.* New York, Vintage Books, Random
         House.
BLOUNT, James H.
    1913 *The American Occupation of the Philippines, 1898-1912.* New
         York, G. P. Putnam's Sons.
BLUMENTRITT, Ferdinand
    1948 *Diccionario Mitológico de Filipinas,* reprinted and edited in
         Encyclopedia of the Philippines, Vol. 10, "Religion." Zoilo M.
         Galand, editor. Manila, Exequiel Floro.
BRIGGS, C. W.
    1904 "Report," *The Baptist Missionary Magazine.* (July) 224-225.
    1913 *The Progressing Philippines.* Philadelphia, Griffith and Rowland
         Press.
BROWN, Arthur Judson
    1903 *The New Era in the Philippines.* Nashville, Publishing House,
         Methodist Episcopal Church, South.
    1936 *One Hundred Years.* New York, Fleming H. Revell Company.

CADY, John F.
    1964 *Southeast Asia, Its Historical Development.* New York, McGraw-Hill Book Company.
COLE, Fay-Cooper
    1945 *The Peoples of Malaysia.* New York, D. Van Nostrand Company.
CONSERVATIVE BAPTIST FOREIGN MISSION SOCIETY
    1959 Annual Report, Evangelism Committee, Philippine Field.
    1961 to 1968 Annual Report, Executive Committee, Philippine Field.
CONSIDINE, John J., ed.
    1966 *The Religious Dimension in the New Latin America.* Notre Dame, Indiana, Fides Publishers.
CORNISH, Louis C.
    1942 *The Philippines Calling.* Philadelphia, Dorrance and Company.
CORPUS, Severino Fermin
    1951 "Social Change in the Philippines During the Independence Movement: 1898-1935." An unpublished Ph.D. dissertation, University of Southern California, Sociology.
CORPUZ, Onofre D.
    1965 *The Philippines.* Englewood Cliffs, New Jersey, Prentice-Hall.
COWAN, Marion M.
    1962 "A Christian Movement in Mexico," *Practical Anthropology.* 9:193-204.
COXILL, H. Wakelin and GRUBB, Kenneth G., eds.
    1962 *World Christian Handbook – 1962.* London, World Dominion Press.
    1968 *World Christian Handbook – 1968.* London, World Dominion Press.
CRAIG, Austin
    1913 *Lineage, Life and Labors of Jose Rizal.* Manila, Philippine Education Company.
CUTSHALL, Alden
    1964 *The Philippines: Nation of Islands.* New York, D. Van Nostrand Company.
DEAN, John Marvin
    1902 *The Cross of Christ in Bolo Land.* Chicago, Fleming H. Revell Company.
DEATS, Richard L.
    1964 *The Story of Methodism in the Philippines.* Manila, National Council of Churches in the Philippines.
DE LA COSTA, H., S. J.
    1961 *The Jesuits in the Philippines 1581-1781.* Cambridge, Mass., Harvard University Press.
    1965 *Readings in Philippine History.* Manila, Bookmark.
DENNIS, James S. *et al.,* eds.
    1911 *World Atlas of Christian Missions.* New York, Student Volunteer Movement for Foreign Missions.
DICKINSON, Robert E.
    1964 *City and Region.* London, Routledge and Kegan Paul.

DIRIGE, Perla V.
    1966 "The Development of Inter-denominational Missions in the
         Philippines." An unpublished MRE thesis, Fuller Theological
         Seminary.
DORN, Luis
    1967 "Philippine Language Trends," *Practical Anthropology.* (July-
         August) 174-185.
DOZIER, Edward P.
    1967 *The Kalinga of Northern Luzon, Philippines.* New York, Holt,
         Rinehart and Winston.
EGGAN, Fred
    1956 *Area Handbook on the Philippines,* 4 vols. University of Chicago
         for the Human Relations Area Files, Preliminary Edition.
ELWOOD, Douglas J.
    1967 "Contemporary Churches and Sects in the Philippines," *The
         South East Asia Journal of Theology.* (October) 56-78.
ESLAO, Nena
    1966 "The Developmental Cycle of the Philippine Household in an
         Urban Setting," *Philippine Sociological Review.* 14:199-208.
ESPERANZA, Trinidad C.
    1965 "The Assemblies of God in the Philippines." An unpublished
         MRE thesis, Fuller Theological Seminary.
FAGG, John Edwin
    1963 *Latin America, A General History.* New York, Macmillan
         Company.
FELIX, Alfonso, Jr.
    1966 *The Chinese in the Philippines 1570-1770,* Vol. 1. Manila,
         Solidaridad Publishing House.
FOREMAN, John
    1906 *The Philippine Islands.* New York, Charles Scribner's Sons.
FOX, Robert B.
    1955a "Culture History," Chapter 4 *in* Eggan's *Area Handbook on the
          Philippines.* 1:250-262.
    1955b "Social Organization," Chapter 8 *in* Eggan's *Area Handbook on
          the Philippines.* 1:413-470.
FRIEND, Theodore
    1965 *Between Two Empires.* New Haven, Yale University Press.
GABRIEL, Remegio B. and Corazon I.
    1968 Interview with author, January 12, 1968.
GALANG, Zoilo M.. ed.
    1950 "Religion," *Encyclopedia of the Philippines,* Vol. 10. Manila,
         Exequiel Floro.
GARCIA, Dolores G.
    1964 "Felix Manalo: The Man and His Mission." *Pasugo,* July
         27:179-183.
GINSBURG, Norton S.
    1955 "The Great City in Southeast Asia," *American Journal of
         Sociology.* (March) 455-462.

GLOVER, Robert Hall, rev. by KANE, J. Herbert
  1960 *The Progress of World-Wide Missions.* New York, Harper & Row.
GONZALES, Mary A.
  1965 "The Ilongo Kinship System and Terminology," *Philippine Sociological Review.* (January) 23-31.
GOWING, Peter G.
  1967 *Islands Under the Cross.* Manila, National Council of Churches in the Philippines.
GRUBB, Kenneth G., and BINGLE, E. J.
  1949 *World Christian Handbook.* London, World Dominion Press.
GRUNDER, Garel A. and LIVEZEY, William F.
  1951 *The Philippines and the United States.* Norman, University of Oklahoma Press.
HOLLISTER, John N.
  1956 *The Centenary of the Methodist Church in Southern Asia.* Lucknow, India, Lucknow Publishing House.
HOLLNSTEINER, Mary R.
  1963 *The Dynamics of Power in a Philippine Municipality.* Quezon City, Community Development Research Council, University of the Philippines.
HUNT, Chester L., *et al.*
  1963 *Sociology in the Philippine Setting.* Revised Edition. Quezon City, Phoenix Publishing House.
ILAGAN, Andres Salcedo
  1968 Interview with author, January 12, 1968.
ISIDRO, Gadiel
  1966 "Area Report: Far East/Pacific." in *The Church's Worldwide Mission.* Harold Lindsell, ed. Texas, Word Books.
JOCANO, F. Landa
  1966 "Cultural Context of Folk Medicine: Some Philippine Cases," *Philippine Sociological Review.* (January) 40-48.
KAST, Edward L.
  1963 "Comments on Church, Plaza and Market Place," *Practical Anthropology.* 10:175-178.
KEESING, Felix M.
  1962 *The Ethnohistory of Northern Luzon.* Stanford, Calif., Stanford University Press.
  1965 *Cultural Anthropology: The Science of Custom.* New York, Holt, Rinehart and Winston.
KEESING, Felix M. and KEESING, Marie
  1934 *Taming Philippine Headhunters.* Stanford, Calif., Stanford University Press.
KROEBER, A. L.
  1918 *The History of Philippine Civilization as Reflected in Religious Nomenclature.* New York, American Museum of Natural History.
  1928 *Peoples of the Philippines.* New York, American Museum of Natural History.
  1948 *Anthropology.* New York, Harcourt, Brace & Company.

LARSON, Donald M.
    1963 "Church, Plaza, and the Market Place," *Practical Anthropology*.
          10:167-174.
LATOURETTE, Kenneth Scott
    1939 *A History of the Expansion of Christianity*. 7 vols. New York,
          Harper & Brothers.
    1962 *Christianity in a Revolutionary Age*. 5 vols. New York, Harper &
          Row.
LAUBACH, Frank Charles
    1925 *The People of the Philippines*. New York, George H. Doran
          Company.
    1936 *Rizal: Man and Martyr*. Manila, Community Publishers.
LEEDER, Leo L.
    1956 "A Survey of Pagan Tribes in the Philippines and of Missionary
          Efforts Toward Their Evangelization." An unpublished M.A.
          thesis, Columbia Bible College.
LERRIGO, P. H. J.
    1903 "The Philippine National Church," *The Baptist Missionary
          Magazine*. (September) 642-643.
LIEBAN, Richard W.
    1967 *Cebuano Sorcery: Malign Magic in the Philippines*. Berkeley,
          University of California Press.
LINDSELL, Harold, ed.
    1966 *The Church's Worldwide Mission*. Waco, Texas, Word Books.
LOPEZ, Fernandez
    1894 *La Religion de los Antiguos Indios Tagalos*. de Los Rios, Madrid,
          Imp. de La Viuda de M. Minuesa.
LUND, Eric
    1900 "Letter," *The Baptist Missionary Magazine*. (September) 526.
    1908 "Letter," *The Baptist Missionary Magazine*. (May) 214.
LUZBETAK, Louis J.
    1963 *The Church and Cultures*. Techny, Illinois, Divine Word Publica-
          tions.
LYNCH, Frank, S. J.
    1955 "Organized Religion in the Philippines," Chapter 9 *in* Eggan's
          Handbook of the Philippines. 2:471-744.
MAJUL, Cesar Adib
    1960 *Mabini and the Philippine Revolution*. Quezon City, University of
          the Philippines.
MALCOLM, George A. and KALAW, Maximo M.
    1932 *Philippine Government*. Boston, D. C. Heath and Company.
    1951 *First Malayan Republic*. Boston, Christopher Publishing House.
MCGAVRAN, Donald Anderson
    1955 *The Bridges of God*. New York, Friendship Press.
    1958a "The Independent Church in the Philippines," *Encounter*.
          (Summer) 299-321.
    1958b *Multiplying Churches in the Philippines*. Manila, United Church
          of Christ in the Philippines.
    1959 *How Churches Grow*. London, World Dominion.

1963 "Review of Struggle for Freedom by Lewis Bliss Whittemore," *Encounter*. (Spring) 258-259.

MCHALE, Thomas R.
1966 "A Modern Corporation Looks at the Philippine Economy and Society in Transition," *Philippine Sociological Review*. (October) 226-231.

MEDNICK, Melvin
1965 *Encampment of the Lake: The Social Organization of a Moslem-Philippine (Moro) People*. Chicago, Philippine Studies Program, Department of Anthropology, University of Chicago.

THE METHODIST CHURCH
1951 to 1955 *General Minutes of the Annual Conference*.

THE METHODIST EPISCOPAL CHURCH
1917 to 1941 *Minutes of the Annual Conference*.

THE MISSIONARY REVIEW OF THE WORLD
1904 Vol. 27, January to December.
1905 Vol. 28, January to December.
1910 Vol. 33, January to December.

MURDOCK, George Peter
1949 *Social Structure*. New York, Macmillan Company.

MURDOCK, George Peter, ed.
1960 *Social Structure in Southeast Asia*. New York, Wenner Gren Foundation for Anthropological Research, Inc.

NEILL, Stephen
1964 *Christian Missions*. Middlesex, England, Penguin Books.

NIDA, Eugene A.
1960 *Message and Mission*. New York, Harper & Row.

NURGE, Ethel
1965 *Life in a Leyte Village*. Seattle, University of Washington Press.

NYDEGGER, William F. and NYDEGGER, Corinne
1966 *Tarong: An Ilocos Barrio in the Philippines*. New York, John Wiley and Sons.

OSIAS, Camilo
1948 *Jose Rizal: His Life and Times*. Manila, Oscal Educational Publishers.

PAL, Agaton Palen
1956 "A Philippine Barrio: A Study of Social Organization in Relation to Planned Cultural Change." An unpublished Ph.D. dissertation, Cornell University.
1963 *The Resources, Level of Living, and Aspirations of Rural Households in Negros Oriental*. Quezon City, Community Development Research Council, University of the Philippines.
1966 "Aspects of Lowland Philippine Social Structure," *Philippine Sociological Review*. (January) 31-40.

PALAZON, Juan
1964 *Majayjay (How a Town Came Into Being)*. Manila, Historical Conservation Society.

PALMA, Rafael
    1949 *The Pride of the Malay Race.* New York, Prentice-Hall. (Translated by Roman Ozaeta from the original Spanish).
PARKER, Joseph I., ed.
    1938 *Interpretative Statistical Survey of the World Mission of the Christian Church.* New York, International Missionary Council.
PARR, Charles McKew
    1964 *Ferdinand Magellan, Circumnavigator.* New York, Thomas Y. Crowell Company.
PASUGO
    1964 Tanging Bilang, July 27.
PHELAN, John Leddy
    1959 *The Hispanization of the Philippines.* Madison, University of Wisconsin Press.
POPULATION REFERENCE BUREAU
    1968 "World Population Data Sheet – 1968."

QUEZON, Manuel Luis
    1946 *The Good Fight.* New York, D. Appleton-Century Company.

RAUSA-GOMEZ, Lourdes
    1967 "Sri Vijaya and Madjapahit," *Philippine Studies.* (January) 63-105.
RAVENHOLT, Albert
    1962 *The Philippines: A Young Republic on the Move.* Princeton, New Jersey, D. Van Nostrand Company.
REDFIELD, Robert
    1960 *The Little Community and Peasant Society and Culture.* Chicago, University of Chicago Press.
REGAN, Joseph W.
    1957 *The Philippines: Christian Bulwark in Asia.* New York, Maryknoll Publications.
REYNOLDS, Harriet R.
    1962 "The Filipino Family in its Cultural Setting," *Practical Anthropology.* 9:223-234.
RIZAL, Jose
    1956a *The Social Cancer (Noli Me Tangere).* Manila, Philippine Education Company (translated by Charles E. Derbyshire from the original Spanish).
    1956b *The Reign of Greed (El Filibusterismo).* Manila, Philippine Education Company (translated by Charles E. Derbyshire from the original Spanish).
RODGERS, James B.
    1940 *Forty Years in the Philippines.* New York, The Board of Foreign Missions of the Presbyterian Church in the United States of America.
ROMULO, Carlos P.
    1955 *Crusade in Asia.* New York, John Day Company.
RUIZ, Leopoldo Teodoseo
    1942 "Development and Solution of Certain Socio-Economic Prob-

lems of the Philippines With Special References to the Present Cooperative Movement." Unpublished Ph.D. dissertation, University of Southern California.

RUSSELL, Charles E. and RODRIGUEZ, E. B.
1923   *The Hero of the Filipinos.* New York, Century Company.

SAN AUGUSTIN
1965   *The Christianization of the Philippines.* Historical Conservative Society and University of San Augustin.

SCAFF, Alvin H.
1955   *The Philippine Answer to Communism.* Stanford, Calif., Stanford University Press.

SHARP, Andrew
1961   *Adventurous Armada.* Christchurch, N.Z., Whitcombe and Tombs Ltd.

SHEARER, Roy E.
1966   *Wildfire: Church Growth in Korea.* Grand Rapids, Eerdmans.

SITOY, Valentino T., Jr.
1967   "Nineteenth Century Evangelical Beginnings in the Philippines," *The South East Asia Journal of Theology.* (October) 42-55.

SOBREPENA, Enrique C.
n.d.   *That They May Be One.* Manila, United Church of Christ in the Philippines.

STEVENSON, Dwight E.
1955   *Christianity in the Philippines.* Lexington, Kentucky, College of the Bible.

STUCKI, Curtis W.
1963   *American Doctoral Dissertation on Asia, 1933-1962.* Ithaca, New York, Cornell University.

STUNTZ, Homer C.
1904a *The Philippines and the Far East.* Cincinnati, Jennings and Pye.
1904b "Past and Present in the Philippines," *The Missionary Review of the World.* (July) 485-493.

TARUC, Luis
1953   *Born of the People.* New York, International Publishers.

TIPPETT, A. R.
1967   *Solomon Islands Christianity.* New York, Friendship Press.

TOLENTINO, Arturo M. and ZAIDE, Gregorio F.
1946   *The Government of the Republic of the Philippines.* Manila, R. P. Garcia Publishing Company.

UNITED CHURCH OF CHRIST IN THE PHILIPPINES
1963   *Year Book.*
1965   *Year Book.*
1968   *Year Book.*

UNITED STATES BUREAU OF CENSUS
1905   *Census of the Philippine Islands 1903.* Washington, D.C.

UNITED STATES SENATE
1902   "Hearings Before the Committee on the Philippines," Senate Document No. 331, 3 parts.

VANDERKROEF, Justus M.
    1966   "Patterns of Cultural Conflict in Philippine Life," *Pacific Affairs.*
           (Fall and Winter) 326-338.
VILLANUEVA, Pedro Reyes
    1964   "Ang Iglesia Ni Cristo Sa Pilipinas Pagkatapos Ng Limampung
           Taon," *Pasugo.* (July) 21-26.
WERNSTEDT, Frederick L. and SPENCER, J. E.
    1967   *The Philippine Island World, A Physical, Cultural, and Regional
           Geography.* Berkeley, University of California Press.
WHITTEMORE, Lewis Bliss
    1961   *Struggle for Freedom.* Greenwich, Conn., Seabury Press.
WINTER, Ralph D.
    1967   *The Extension Seminary and the Programmed Textbook, A
           Report of a Workshop, Armenia, Colombia, Sept. 4-9, 1967.*
           Pasadena, Calif., Fuller Theological Seminary.
WOLFF, Leon
    1961   *Little Brown Brother.* London, Longmans.
WORCESTER, Dean C.
    1899   *The Philippine Islands and Their People.* New York, Macmillan
           Company.
YOUNGHUSBAND, Major G. J.
    1899   *The Philippines and Round About.* New York, Macmillan
           Company.
ZAIDE, Gregorio F.
    n.d.   *Political and Social History of the Philippines.* 2 vols., Manila,
           Mimeo. Garcia Book Store.
    1939   *History of the Katipunan.* Manila, Loyal Press.
    1958   *Philippine History for High Schools.* Manila, Modern Book
           Company.

INDEX